Fifty Hikes in Connecticut

Fifty Hikes in Connecticut

Short Walks and Day Hikes Around the Nutmeg State

THIRD EDITION

Gerry and Sue Hardy

Photographs by the Authors

A Fifty Hikes™ Guide

Backcountry Publications
Woodstock, Vermont

The trail could use some clearing, but it's well blazed!

Acknowledgments

Many of our thoughts were honed on our numerous hiking companions, to whom we are very grateful. The Appalachian Mountain Club groups we hike with provide an endless supply of wit and good fellowship.

Above all, we would like to thank the dedicated chairmen of the Connecticut Forest and Park Association for the existence and maintenance of Connecticut's Blue Trails, members of the Connecticut Chapter of the AMC for maintaining the Appalachian Trail in Connecticut, and all those who laid out and maintain the many other fine trails in our state.

For their help in the preparation of the third edition, we want to thank Mary Anne Hardy, Patty Hardy, Steve Henniger, and especially Joyce Don, who walked so many miles with us for this revision.

An Invitation to the Reader

Over time trails can be rerouted and signs and landmarks altered. If you find that changes have occurred on the routes described in this book, please let us know so that corrections may be made in future editions. The author and publisher also welcome other comments and suggestions. Address all correspondence to:

Editor, *Fifty Hikes*™ Series
Backcountry Publications
P.O. Box 175
Woodstock, VT 05091

© 1978, 1984, 1991 by Gerry and Sue Hardy
All rights reserved
Printed in the United States of America
Published by Backcountry Publications, a division of
The Countryman Press, Inc., Woodstock, Vermont 05091

Third edition: fourth printing, 1994

Text and cover design by Wladislaw Finne
Trail maps drawn by Richard Widhu

Photograph on page 38 by Nancy-Jane Jackson. Photograph on page 83 by Lawrence S. Millard. All other photographs by the authors.

Cover: *View from Bear Mountain* by Roland Normand

Library of Congress Cataloging-in-Publication Data

Hardy, Gerry.
    Fifty hikes in Connecticut: short walks and day hikes around the
  Nutmeg State / Gerry and Sue Hardy; photographs by the authors—
  3rd ed.
      p. cm.
  Includes bibliographical references (p.).
  ISBN 0-88150-151-4
    1. Hiking—Connecticut—Guide-books. 2. Connecticut—Description
and travel—1981- —Guide-books. I. Hardy, Sue II. Title.
III. Title: 50 hikes in Connecticut.
GV199.42.C8H37 1991
917.46'0443—dc20   90-25196
                                                 CIP

To David, Chuck, and Patty—as always. We also dedicate this new edition to a new addition, our grandson Nicholas Bujalski, and his parents Mary Anne Hardy and Phil Bujalski.

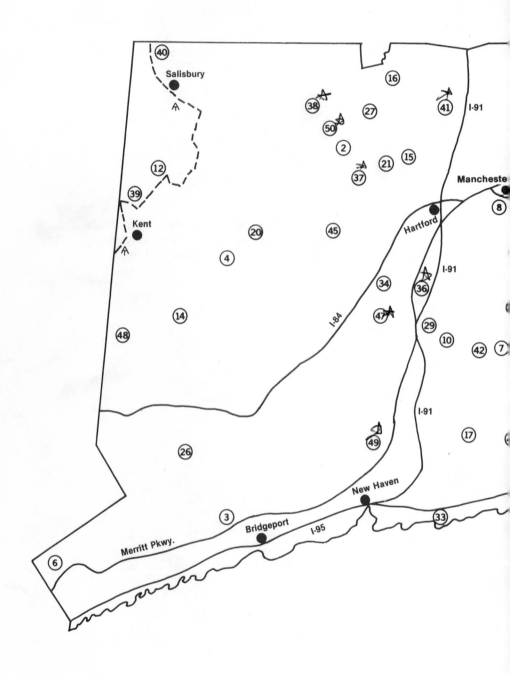

Contents

Introduction   9
Introduction to the Third Edition   14
Further Reading   17

Half-Day Hikes

1.   Oak Grove   20
2.   Great Pond   24
3.   Larsen Sanctuary   27
4.   Mount Tom Tower   30
5.   Gillette Castle   33
6.   Greenwich Audubon Sanctuary   36
7.   Hurd State Park   40
8.   Highland Springs and Lookout Mountain   43
9.   Rocky Neck   47
10.   Wadsworth Falls   50
11.   Nayantaquit Trail   53
12.   Pine Knob Loop   56
13.   Day Pond Loop   59
14.   Sunny Valley   63
15.   Northwest Park   67
16.   Newgate Prison   70
17.   Chatfield Hollow   73
18.   Soapstone Mountain   77
19.   Bluff Point   81
20.   White Memorial Foundation   84
21.   Penwood   89
22.   Mount Misery   92
23.   Gay City   96
24.   Green Falls Pond   100
25.   Wolf Den   104
26.   Collis P. Huntington State Park   108
27.   McLean Game Refuge   112
28.   Great Hill   116
29.   Mount Higby   120
30.   Northern Nipmuck   123
31.   Natchaug   127
32.   Bullet and High Ledges   130
33.   Westwoods   134
34.   Ragged Mountain Loop   138

18

I-84

ckville

I-384
46

30
31   25
43

Willimantic

Connecticut Tpke.
I-395

13

Norwich

22

24

35

32

5
11

I-95

New London

9

19

All-Day Hikes

35. Devil's Hopyard   144
36. Chauncey Peak and Mount Lamentation   149
37. Heublein Tower   152
38. People's Forest   155
39. Macedonia Brook   158
40. Bear Mountain Loop   161
41. Windsor Locks Canal   165
42. Seven Falls   168
43. Mansfield Hollow   171
44. Cockaponset   174
45. Tunxis Ramble   178
46. Bolton Notch Railroad   181
47. West Peak and Castle Crag   185
48. Housatonic Range   188
49. Sleeping Giant   191
50. Ratlum Mountain and Indian Caves   196

Introduction

Contrary to popular opinion, Connecticut is not all city and suburbs. A gratifyingly high proportion of our state's woodland is preserved as state parks and state forests. In fact, the only state in New England with more miles of hiking trails is New Hampshire.

These fifty hikes represent all areas of the state and traverse almost all the existing natural habitats. Naturally, this selection is only a sampler and, of necessity, somewhat reflects our own preferences and prejudices. We chose the hikes with an eye to the hiking family; most are suitable for families with young children (who are usually far more capable physically than psychologically). But remember, a hike adults and teenagers can cover in four hours may take all day with youngsters along, especially if they take time to examine their surroundings closely.

We have written this book to please both the armchair hiker and the trail walker by fleshing out directions with photographs and snippets of natural history. We have also tried to answer some of the questions the average hiker might ask while walking these trails. The phenomena we describe we actually saw on these fifty hikes; by being fairly observant you can see the same things. For this reason our descriptions are short on wildlife, which is seen only occasionally, and long on vegetation and terrain. Effective observation of animal life requires very slow movement (if any), blinds, and binoculars or scopes. In contrast, vegetation and terrain features require only an alert eye and an inquiring mind.

These hikes, which we feel represent some of the most attractive of the state's trails, break longer trails into palatable chunks that can be completed in a specified period of time. In addition to some of the best pieces of the Blue Trail system, finest stretches of Connecticut's section of the Appalachian Trail (AT), and more interesting state park trail systems, we have included a few hikes in wildlife sanctuaries and city- and town-owned, open-space areas.

Choosing a Hike

The hikes are presented in order of their overall difficulty; the first hike, Oak Grove, is the easiest, and the last one, Ratlum Mountain, the most difficult. However, since difficulty is averaged over an entire hike, many of the later hikes have quite easy sections. The book is broken into two parts for your convenience: half-day hikes and all-day hikes. While the half-day hikes can be completed by many hikers in three hours or less, trying to complete an all-day hike in an afternoon may cause you to miss supper.

Total Distance is the mileage walked if you complete the entire hike as described. Many of these hikes lend themselves readily to shortening if you desire an easier day. Trail distances are given in fractions of a mile for some hikes and in decimals for others. Fractional distances are estimates, while decimal distances have usually been measured with a wheel and are quite accurate.

Hiking time is computed from a simple formula used all over the country: two miles an hour plus one-half hour for every 1,000 feet of vertical rise. Thus, a six-mile hike on flat terrain would have a three-hour hiking time, but a six-mile hike with 2,000 feet of climbing would take four hours. If you are middle-aged and a beginning hiker you probably won't match "book time" for a while. A young, experienced hiker will consistently better these times. One word of caution — hiking time means just that and does not allow for lunch stops, rest stops, sightseeing, or picture taking.

The *rating* for each hike refers to the average difficulty of the terrain you traverse on the route we have described. The difficulty of a hike is relative. A tough section in Connecticut is far easier than a tough section in New Hampshire or Vermont. Our rating system is the one used by the Connecticut Chapter of the Appalachian Mountain Club and is designed for Connecticut trails. It combines such factors as elevation gain, rock scrambling, footpath condition, and steepness. Hikes rated D are the easiest and A the most difficult. The seven categories used in our rating system are:

D.   Flat terrain; little or no elevation change, easy footing
CD. Intermediate between C and D
C.   Average terrain; moderate ups-and-downs with some need to watch footing
CB. Intermediate between C and B
B.   Difficult terrain; steep climbs, considerable elevation gain or some poor footing or both
AB. Intermediate between A and B

A.   Very tough terrain; maximum elevation gain, poor footing or hand-assisted scrambling up steep pitches or both

When selecting a day's ramble, don't overdo it. If you haven't hiked before, try the shorter, easier hikes first and build up to the longer ones gradually. Don't bite off more than you can chew — that takes all the pleasure out of hiking. As the saying goes, "walk till you're half tired out, then turn around and walk back."

Highlights are not just teasers to attract you to a particular hike. Used properly they should help you choose a hike on the basis of weather and the proclivities of your companions. On clear, cool days distant viewpoints are in order. Youngsters like nature museums, scrambling over rocks, and swimming. Hot days call for cool, flat, woods walks.

About Connecticut Seasons

Hiking in Connecticut is a four-season avocation. Our winters are relatively mild — we rarely have temperatures below zero Fahrenheit or snow accumulations over a foot. In general, the snow deepens and the temperature drops as you travel north and west. Often the southeastern part of the state is snow-free much of the winter and is the first area in the state to experience spring.

Spring is usually wet and muddy, although there is frequently a dry period of high fire danger before the trees leaf out. Spring flowers start in April and peak in May. Days of extreme heat in the nineties can come anytime in late spring.

The humid heat of summer demands short, easy, early morning strolls. Beginners often think summer is the best time to hike; veterans consider it the worst time! However, in summer the foliage is lush and botanizing at its best.

Fall is the ideal hiking season. Cool, crisp days make us forget the enervating heat of summer; the colorful foliage and clear air make New England's fall unsurpassed. A better combination of season and place may exist elsewhere, but we doubt it. The color starts with a few shrubs and the bright reds of swamp maples. When other trees start to turn, the swamp maples are bare. Then tree follows tree—sugar maple, ash, birch, beech, and finally oak—turning, blending, fading, falling. There is no better way to enjoy a New England fall than to explore the woods on foot.

How to Hike

We do not mean to tell you how to walk. Most of us have been walking from an early age. Rather, we offer a few hints to help you gain as much pleasure and satisfaction as possible from a hike.

First and most important, wear decent, comfortable footgear that is well broken in. Children can often hike comfortably in good sneakers; adults usually shouldn't. We're heavier and our feet need more support than canvas offers. On the other hand, you don't need heavyweight mountain boots in Connecticut. A lightweight hiking boot or a good work boot with a vibram or lug sole is ideal. While these soles may be hard on the wood trails, we do recommend them as most Connecticut hiking alternates between woods and rocky ledges, where the lug soles are very helpful. Your boots should be worn over two pairs of socks, one lightweight and one heavyweight. Wool or a wool-polypropylene blend is preferable for both pairs as it provides warmth even when wet.

Second, wear comfortable, loose-fitting clothes that don't bind, bunch, or chafe. Cotton T-shirts over a polypropylene mesh shirt are good; synthetics are less comfortable. For our day hikes, except in winter, we favor cut-off jeans or good hiking shorts; they're loose and have lovely pockets for storing a neckerchief, a handkerchief, insect repellent, film, tissues, and a pocket knife.

Establish a comfortable pace that you can maintain for long periods of time. The hiker who charges down the trail not only misses the subtleties of the surroundings but also frequently starts gasping for breath after fifteen minutes or so of hiking. That's no fun! A steady pace lets you see more and cover more ground comfortably than the start-and-stop, huff-and-puff hiker.

When you climb a slope, slow your pace so you can continue to the top without having to stop. (Having to stop is different from choosing to stop at places of interest!) With practice you'll develop an uphill rhythm and find you actually cover ground faster by going slowly.

Many veteran hikers use a restful step in which they lock the knee the weight is on, letting the other leg rest as it swings relaxed from the hip to take the next step. This way each leg rests half the time. An hour of hiking is thus much less tiring than an hour of standing, where neither leg gets to rest.

What to Carry

You may have read articles on the portable household the backpacker carries. While the day hiker needn't shoulder this burden, there are some things you should carry to assure a comfortable and safe hike. Ideally you will always carry your emergency gear and never use it. Items 2-10 below live in our day packs:

1. Small, comfortable, lightweight pack.

2. First-aid kit containing at least adhesive bandages, moleskin (for incipient blisters), scissors, adhesive tape, gauze pads, aspirin, salt tablets, ace bandage, and bacitracin. We always carry both elastic knee and ankle braces and Ace bandages—we have used them more than any of our other first-aid equipment.

3. Wool or polypro shirt or sweater and a lightweight, nylon windbreaker. A fast-moving cold front can turn a balmy spring day into a blustery snow-spitting disaster, and sun-warmed, sheltered valleys may contrast sharply with elevated open ledges.

4. Lightweight raingear. In warm, rainy weather, hikers are of two minds about raingear—some don it immediately and get wet from perspiration; others don't and get wet from the rain. In colder weather wear it for warmth. In any case, if the day is threatening it's wise to have dry clothes in the car.

5. Water. Except for occasional springs, water in southern New England is rarely safe to drink. Always carry at least a quart canteen (more on hot summer days) per hiker.

6. Food. In addition to your lunch, carry some high-energy food for emergencies. Gorp—a hand-mixed combination of chocolate chips, nuts, and dried fruit—is good.

7. Flashlight with extra batteries and bulb. You should plan to return to your car before dark, but be prepared in case you're delayed.

8. A well-sharpened pocket knife. This tool has a thousand uses.

9. Map and compass (optional). These items are not necessary for day hikers in Connecticut who stay on well-defined trails and use a guidebook. However, if you want to do any off-trail exploring, you should learn to use a map and compass and carry them with you.

10. Others: toilet paper (always); insect repellent (in season); a hat or sunscreen lotion (on bright days); a wool hat and gloves (in spring and fall).

Winter hiking requires much additional equipment and does not fall within the scope of this book. Nonetheless, it is a lovely time to hike and we would encourage you to hone your skill in mild weather, consult experienced winter hikers, and consider winter's clear, crisp, often snow-white days.

Potpourri

Footing is the major difference between road walking and hiking. Roads present a minimum of obstacles to trip you; at times hiking trails seem to have a maximum. The angular traprock cobbles on many of Connecticut's ridges tend to roll beneath your feet, endangering ankles and balance. An exposed wet root acts as a super banana peel and lichen on wet rock as a lubricant. Stubs of improperly cut bushes are nearly invisible obstacles which trip or puncture. All these potential hazards dictate that you walk carefully on the trail.

It is far safer to hike with a companion than to venture out alone. Should an accident occur while you're alone, you're in trouble. If you must hike alone, be sure someone knows where you are, your exact route, and when you plan to return.

While hiking, don't litter. The AMC motto "Carry In—Carry Out" is a good one. Carry a small plastic bag in your pack for garbage. When it comes to human waste, head well off the trail and stay at least two hundred feet from any water. Be sure to bury any wastes and toilet paper. Leave the woods as you found them.

On any hike, the vegetation you see has been left unpicked by previous trekkers. You, in turn, should leave all plants for the next hiker to admire. This courtesy applies not only to the wanton picker, but also to the scientific collector. If you must collect, do it away from the trails and off state land. Remember to "take only pictures; leave only footprints."

Connecticut has a limited-liability law to protect landowners who grant access to the general public free of charge. This saves property owners from capricious lawsuits and opens up more private lands for trails.

Hiking should be much more than a walk in the woods. Knowledge of natural and local history adds another dimension to your rambles. We dip lightly into these areas to give you a sampling to whet an inquiring mind. To aid further investigation, we offer a short descriptive Further Reading section following the Introduction to the Third Edition. Good field guides in your pack will add immeasurably to a hike.

The Connecticut 400 Club

Many hikers collect attractive patches to signify completion of a goal. The AMC sponsors, among others, the New Hampshire 4000-Footers Club and the New England 4000-Footers Club for those who have climbed the forty-seven mountains in New Hampshire or the sixty-four in northern New England that are over 4,000 feet high. Special patches are awarded to applicants for a small fee.

Connecticut's peaks are less lofty. However, the Connecticut Chapter of the AMC has since 1976 sponsored the Connecticut 400 Club whose members have hiked all the "Through Trails" (approximately 450 miles) described in the *Connecticut Walk Book*. Patches are awarded to applicants for a small fee. The Connecticut 400 Club was established not only to recognize those who have hiked the through trails but, perhaps more importantly, to encourage hikers to explore all the trails in the state, thus reducing traffic on the famous but overused Appalachian Trail.

For the name and address of the current Connecticut 400 Patch chairman or for information on the Connecticut Chapter of the AMC, write to the Appalachian Mountain Club, 5 Joy St., Boston, MA 02108.

Day packs showing the Connecticut 400 patch

Introduction to the Third Edition

Revising a hiking guide is a never-ending task. A new edition becomes necessary when steadily accumulating discrepancies no longer justify the automatic reprinting of the old edition. Outdated hiking guides can be particularly frustrating for new hikers.

The time has come for a second major revision. Due to accumulated changes in vegetative growth, forest cutting, and storm damage, as well as the inexorable spread of development, several hikes from the second edition have been deleted. Cathedral Pines, a 200-year-old white pine grove—the oldest in New England—was devastated by a tornado on July 10, 1989. Eventually, this land, now owned by the Nature Conservancy, will be reopened for hiking. Dean Ravine and Barrack Mountain have been deleted due to an Appalachian Trail relocation, and Mohawk Mountain was also severely damaged in the aforementioned tornado. Major changes were required for several other hikes, and virtually none of our hike writeups emerged unscathed. A good example of this is Hike 44 (Cockaponset): about the time the second edition hit the bookstores the named access road (Filley) was closed and the trailhead could only be reached via Cedar Lake Road.

A new, carefully written trail book is ideal for the beginner, but as the years pass, more and more trail descriptions vary from the original until only the experienced and woods-wise hiker finds the book useful. Eventually, early editions become the cherished possessions of only the history-minded hiker. Among our personal mementos are an 1859 second edition of *Eastman's White Mountain Guide,* a 1932 edition of *Walks and Rides in Central Connecticut and Massachusetts,* a 1937 first edition of the *Connecticut Walk Book,* and a 1923 set of detailed maps of the Long Trail in Vermont. With such books and maps, you can trace the development of a trail or of an area. It is possible, for example, to reconstruct much of the Long Path, which Native Americans and early settlers once used to travel from the Boston area to and through Connecticut. This adds another dimension to hiking that makes it more than mere exercise.

Another fascinating aspect of hiking involves observing and considering your environment. Think about why some plants are found in the southern but not in the northern part of Connecticut. Also, what role do the ancient plants—ferns, mosses, and lichens—play? Why are our woods lined with old roads and dotted with cellar holes? Why do some trees grow straight and tall, while others have outflung low branches? Someone once said that "ecology is more complicated than you think; in fact, it is more complicated than you can think!" You will never run out of things to learn on your hikes! In our own trail descriptions we have thrown in a smattering of natural history. We've only touched on a few things, and we've tried not to repeat ourselves from hike to hike. Much of what we see and describe on one hike also exists on many of the others.

Every Eden has its serpent. Connecticut's, in warm weather, is its tiny biting pests. We've all seen horror pictures of hikers in the far north, with their shirts blackened with blood-sucking mosquitos. Explorers of the tropics fear not lions or tigers but biting insects most of all. In Connecticut, you can avoid this problem by hiking in the winter or on chilly fall and spring days (which are often ideal for hiking). For your summer excursions, understanding the problem and knowing its appropriate remedies will greatly enhance your enjoyment.

The mosquito, the dog tick, the deer fly, and the black fly are old "friends." In the last decade or so we have added two more pests as well that merit our attention — water-borne *giardia* and Lyme Disease (carried by the deer tick). Mosquitos can be kept at bay with most good insect repellents. The major problem with repellents is that in warm weather they will be washed away by perspiration, thus requiring reapplication from time to time. You will know when this time comes when the hovering insects start landing and biting. The dog tick has never been a problem for us personally despite thousands of hours of hiking. We have picked off a few from our clothes after our passing warmth prompted them to hitch a ride; however, these ticks have never dug in. Conversely, our family dog was very susceptible to them, and we would usually discover their blood-swollen bodies nestled in the fur while petting the dog. Occasionally little children will pick them up — they can often be found amid the hairs at the nape of their necks.

The deer fly is another common pest in the summer. This housefly-sized insect tends to buzz around the back of your head, temporarily land on your hair, and, if undisturbed, dig in. Fortunately, if you pay some attention you'll easily catch and kill them. The black fly can be a horrendous pest farther north. However, they last only a short time in Connecticut and in our experiece don't present a major problem to adults here. A few years ago conventional wisdom stated that despite exorbitant claims no insect repellent would work against them. Since then, repellents containing 90%+ DEET have been found to be effective against all insect pests. They have become our repellents of choice.

Despite sensational coverage in the newspapers, the two "new" diseases can also be understood and foiled. The easiest to handle is the trophozoite — *giardia*. Warmblooded creatures (like us) ingest tiny *giardia* cysts (about 16,500 can fit on the head of a pin) from contaminated drinking water. In the gut, they will hatch, multiply, attach to the upper small intestine, and then do their damage, which can include diarrhea, cramps, and visible bloating. The cysts infest many warmblooded animals including the now numerous beavers, and they easily spread from stream to stream via infected animals. Once in a water supply they are usually there for good. Therefore, never drink untreated water! This means carrying your own water while day hiking and properly treating your drinking water while backpacking. In many states *giardia* has become established in town water supplies, which causes wholesale infections. Once correctly diagnosed, however, it is easily treated.

Lyme Disease was named for a Connecticut town near Long Island Sound where it was first identified in 1975. Carried by the very small deer tick (only ¼″ diameter even when fully engorged with blood), Lyme Disease does not affect most animals other than humans except for dogs, who may develop joint disorders. This illness is now the United States' most prevalent tick-borne illness, and the number of cases increases yearly. Originally reported only in southern New England, it has been found (using different tick carriers in different regions of the world) in forty-three states and on all continents except Antarctica. European literature almost a century ago reported a similar group of symptoms. Its dissemination may have been helped by the modern air liner and similar forces that are "shrinking" the globe. To paraphrase Matthew Hart in the July 1990 issue of *Atlantic* magazine (p. 86), "The extension of [any living creature] is part of what some biologists describe as the homogenization of the planet — a process both inevitable and inexorable, as species after species casts itself abroad." Fortunately only 10-65% of all deer ticks are infected, so the chances of getting bitten are not high for hikers and other outdoorsmen (suburbanites seem much more susceptible). Proper treatment within a few weeks of infection is also very effective. While rarely fatal, untreated Lyme Disease produces debilitating symptoms that can persist for a lifetime. Within a month of infection, a circular rash a few inches in diameter usually encircles the tick bite location. Even at this stage, the illness is treatable with antibiotics. The Audubon article referred to in Further Readings states, "For now, experts say the best way to protect yourself against Lyme Disease is to wear long sleeves, tuck in your trousers, use tick repellent on clothing, and check yourself for ticks. If you have been bitten, contact a physician. No matter where you live, keep an eye out for [deer] ticks. Lyme disease isn't going to go away, nor are the ticks." To put things in a reasonable perspective, we know literally hundreds of hikers, most of whom live in the northeast. We only know of four who have ever had Lyme Disease, and one of them has had it

three times — all before he started hiking! He's sure he got it working in his garden.

Hiking trails do not just happen for our healthy enjoyment, and, as we in Connecticut are well aware, they are impermanent at best. When the first *Connecticut Walk Book* was published in 1937, all the major trails in Connecticut were interconnected. The pressures of change have long since isolated most of these trails from each other. The major reason we still have good hiking trails is that hikers like rough, hard-to-reach land for their hikes, while builders prefer easily developed land. However, as time passes and populations grow, the hiker's land becomes more and more endangered. Let's examine the history of the Appalachian Trail (AT), which mirrors the problems that beset many hiking trails.

The bane of the hiker in our uncertain world is the continual loss of hiking trail to development, land use change, or just plain unhappy land owners. The AT had been at the mercy of changes such as these since its inception in the thirties. By the late sixties some 200 miles of this trail, once on private land, were displaced onto paved roads. The volunteer Appalachian Trail Conference located in Harper's Ferry, West Virginia, which coordinated the building and maintenance of the AT, was paying more and more attention to the loss of this "wild" land. Largely because of a major push by volunteers and pressure from the public, the US Congress passed The National Trails System Act which President Johnson signed into law on October 2, 1968. While this potentially made the AT a permanent entity, no money was appropriated at that time to make the dream a reality.

In 1978 the Act was amended, authorizing the National Park Service to acquire a 1000-foot-wide Appalachian Trail corridor on the private land where about half of the original trail was located. Fortunately, Congress also appropriated $90,000,000 to effect the needed acquisitions. As of January 31, l989, 1776 parcels of land totaling 79,624 acres along 522.6 miles of trail had been acquired. However, in 1990 almost 100 miles of trail have yet to be protected — including several hundred parcels of land (30,000 acres) spanning all 14 of the Trail's states. Much has been done, but the toughest acquisitions remain. With the escalating cost of land and the uncertain attitude of recent administrations, it may take yet another decade to complete this very vital public acquisition!

What can we, the hiking public, do about this persistent problem? The hikes in this book are the direct result of efforts of thousands of volunteers like you and me. Most of us do not have the time, ability, or money to make major contributions. However, we can all vote, support conservation-oriented politicians, and do some sort of volunteer trail work. We must work to create an atmosphere of trust and understanding vis-a-vis private landowners. The hiker's cause is damaged by vandalism, rowdiness, and lack of respect for landowners' rights. But we all benefit by courteous hikers, diligent volunteer trail workers, and an understanding of landowners' concerns.

Further Reading

Connecticut is a small state with pleasing outdoor diversity. The hikes in this book touch lightly on many aspects of its ever-fascinating scene: flora, fauna, geology, and history. Since this is basically a hiking book, we have had neither the space nor the time to go into great detail, but we hope we have piqued your interest, so you will want to become more knowledgeable about the outdoors and the history of Connecticut. Although far from being a definitive list, these books and articles should enhance your understanding of Connecticut's outdoors and add to your experience with this book. The following hiking guides are invaluable:

The Appalachian Trail cuts through the northwestern corner of Connecticut and is featured in the *Official Guides* issued by the Appalachian Trail Confer-

ence, PO Box 807, Harper's Ferry, West Virginia 25425.

A precursor to the *Connecticut Walk Books* was *Walks and Rides in Central Connecticut and Massachusetts* by C. R. Longwell and E. S. Dana, The Tuttle, Morehouse, & Taylor Company, New Haven, CT. Since these Yale professors specialized in geology, this book is built around the forces that created and shaped the state's terrain.

Susan Cooley's *Country Walks in Connecticut,* AMC Press, 1982, presents details of several of the Nature Conservancy's holdings from a hiking naturalist's perspective.

Since this corner of the nation is composed of six diverse states, we often think of ourselves as New Englanders. A grounding in all of New England's changes certainly increases our understanding of Connecticut itself. We recommend *Changing Face of New England* by B. F. Thompson, Houghton Mifflin, 1958, *Changes in the Land* by W. Cronin, Hill & Wang, 1983, and *A Guide to New England's Landscape* by Neil Jorgensen, Pequot Press, 1977.

Neil Jorgensen's *A Sierra Club Naturalist Guide to Southern New England,* Sierra Club Books, 1978, examines a narrower section of the northeast in greater detail, thus narrowing the scope while broadening the understanding of our natural wonders.

Many of the Peterson Field Guides are invaluable in identifying the species of natural history met along the trail. Those of special value to us include: *A Field Guide to Wildflowers* by M. McKinney & R. T. Peterson; *A Field Guide to the Mammals* by W. H. Burt & R. P. Grossenheider; *A Field Guide to the Ferns and Their Related Families of Northeastern and Central North America* by B. Cobb; *A Field Guide to the Reptiles and Amphibians of the United States and Canada East of the 100th Meridian* by R. Conant; and *A Field Guide to Trees and Shrubs* by G. A. Petrides.

A special little softcover book just issued, *Connecticut's Notable Trees* by G. D. Dreyer (Memoir of the Connecticut Botanical Society #2 – 1989), not only lists the dimensions and location of all the known largest trees of each species in Connecticut but also several large historic oaks and the largest known specimens of ash, eastern cottonwood, and elms. This is a first edition culled from the findings of a large volunteer project.

If you want to go beyond the "nuts and bolts" of identification, the following books contain much of the lore that is so dear to the hearts of natural history buffs: *How to Know the Ferns* by F. T. Parsons, Dover, 1961; *A Natural History of Trees* by D. C. Peattie, Houghton Mifflin, 1950; *Trees of Eastern and Central United States and Canada* by W. M. Halow, Dover, 1957; and *How to Know the Wildflowers* by W. S. Dana, Dover, 1963.

The forces that shaped our land can also be found in *Underfoot: A Geological Guide to the Appalachian Trail* by V. C. Chew, Appalachian Trail Conference, 1988, which covers the trail's entire 2000 miles, including the trail section that passes through Northwestern Connecticut. Excellent geological coverage of all of Connecticut for the layman is provided by M. Bell's *The Face of Connecticut: The People, Geology, and the Land,* State Geological and Natural History Survey of Connecticut, 1985.

For more on Lyme Disease, see "Something Scary Lurks Out There" by Edward R. Ricciutti, *Audubon* magazine, May 1981, pp. 89-93. *Giardia* is ably presented in "Don't Drink the Water" in the same issue of *Audubon,* pp. 95-97.

Finally, there are several books published on other outdoor aspects of our state. These include *Connecticut Railroads: An Illustrated History,* Connecticut Historical Society, 1986, and *Fishery Survey of the Lakes and Ponds of Connecticut by° the State Board of Fisheries and Game,* The Lake and Pond Survey, 1959.

Half-Day Hikes

Covered bridge at Oak Grove

1

Oak Grove

Total Distance: 1.25 miles
Time: ½ hour
Rating: D
Highlights: Pond, covered bridge
Maps: USGS 7½' Manchester, Rockville

For most of man's existence the natural world has been something to conquer, to overcome, to change to satisfy our needs. Only in the last century has anyone felt any differently. With the English leisured class and their love of mountains, this attitude started to change. On this side of the ocean John Burroughs (closely associated with the Catskills) and John Muir (founder of the Sierra Club) were the among the greatest early proponents of preservation of the natural world. In the very important vanguard of today's conservation movement are the teachers who pass on the wisdom and lore of our natural world to future generations. Thoreau probably said it best when he said "In wilderness is the preservation of the world" (*Walden*).

This idea whose time has come is being disseminated by teachers working in numerous vest-pocket sized sanctuaries across the country. Manchester's Oak Grove Nature Center is such a place. Others include Greenwich Audubon Sanctuary, Larsen Sanctuary and Northwest Park.

During the school year, 43-acre Oak Grove Nature Center is one of many such sites heavily used by teachers. The Nature Center is staffed by two town-paid naturalists who maintain the center and the preserve and assist in the education of the town's children. Oak Grove is used extensively by the town of Manchester and surrounding towns through a cooperative agreement with the water company. The trails are always open for hiking but the building is closed to the general public.

Early summer with its languid lushness is an ideal time to visit this reserve. This very easy hike will not tax you physically, so use a naturalist's approach to derive the most from your visit here. Go slowly and observe your surrounding carefully—you can never go too slowly for nature's sake.

To reach Oak Grove Nature Center, from westbound I-384 take exit 4, Highland Street; at the end of the exit turn left and in .5 mile go right on Autumn Street. From eastbound I-384 take exit 4, Wyllys Street; at the end of the ramp go left across the highway, then go left at the light on Highland Street and in .7 mile go right on Autumn Street. Cross the small bridge and immediately go right on Oak Grove Street. The Nature Center is on your right in .1 mile.

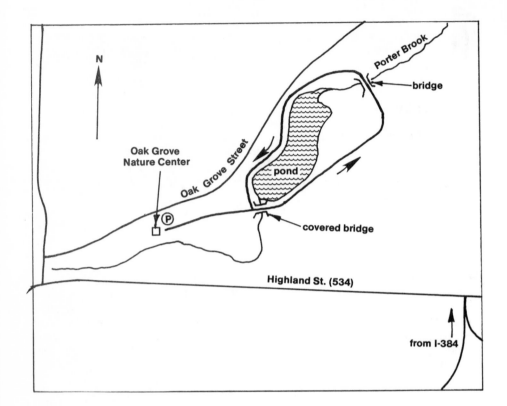

Our trail starts in the corner of the parking lot opposite the center. At first glance you can see this will be an easy hike on a pleasant, well cared for trail. The wide, wood chip strewn path bears right and soon the outlet brook from the pond is seen at right. Shortly where there is a large black birch in the middle of the trail, the path forks. Go right (we'll return on the left fork), and soon you come to another fork. Both trails go to the same place—the right fork goes down along the outlet brook, then climbs stairs up to meet the left fork near the small covered footbridge. The loop trail continues along the earthen dam, while you go right down the stairs to the bridge.

The pond is set in an earthen bowl with a dam containing it. The trees on the wooded banks shade the pond and their branches extend over and almost into the pond. How many shades of green can you see along the pond? Do those shades change much with the season or are they due to the type of tree and the tree's location? This is how to look and think to get the most out of your time outdoors.

Oak Grove has many of the animals commonly found throughout Connecticut, such as deer, raccoons, and opossums. However, in this water-centered preserve, many animals attracted to and sustained by the pond are found. These include mink and muskrat, painted and snapping turtles, spotted salamanders, spring peepers, green, pickerel, bull, and wood frogs, and toads who seek the pond, fill the air for a few days with their swollen-throated trilling, mate, and lay eggs so the next generation can imitate their unseen and unknown parents.

At the end of the bridge stay on the trail near the water's edge; in places the trail jogs up slightly to avoid wet feet. If the water is very high, there is a trail that goes uphill right at the end of the bridge, parallels the pond, and just past a farm field, drops down to rejoin our trail as it swings away from the pond.

After a small boardwalk, at the next fork go left on the blue trail (a red trail goes right), and at the next fork near the swampy end of the pond stay right on the blue-blazed trail. Pass through a small hemlock grove and continue above the inlet stream. Soon the trail enters a darker evergreen forest, so notice the difference here—the forest floor is darker and clear as the hemlocks shade out undergrowth. Less than 100 yards earlier you were in a deciduous forest lush with shrubs and bushes and sunlight. Our blue trail bears left downhill and soon reaches a bridge across the inlet stream.

At the end of the bridge, bear right uphill away from the stream and water-loving hemlocks and at the fork go left, still on the blue trail (the right fork leads up to Oak Grove Street about .5 mile from the nature center).

Soon pass stairs at left leading up from the lower trail and a giant, much-initialed beech tree at right. Tall oaks rise high overhead—notice the recent lightning strike near the base of one left of the trail. The end of the pond appears at left. You may flush a solitary mallard as we did. He evidently felt the center of the pond was safer. Shortly you come to stairs (with railings!) leading to Oak Grove Street. This is a fine spot to play "watcher at the pond." What are those trees, vines, flowers, and bushes? What are those background noises? What causes the wakes, ripples, and ruckuses in the pond? The rattling noise is caused by a kingfisher. The smaller turtles on logs are usually painted turtles. That great form beneath the water is a snapping turtle. The jug-o-rums are from bull frogs. These bits of relevant information are endless.

The covered bridge where you started the loop is visible across the pond. Pass another trail at right leading to the street; continue up the stairs to the earthen dam and proceed past the covered bridge. At the next fork go right and walk down the wooden stairs to rejoin the trail where you started. Retrace your steps to your car.

Great Pond

Total Distance: 1½ miles
Time: ¾ hour
Rating: D
Highlights: Quiet pond
Map: USGS 7½' Tariffville

This hike circles a delightful little body of water paradoxically called Great Pond. You will appreciate short hikes such as this one best when you take them slowly. Adopt a silent, hesitative step to enhance your chances of surprising wildlife. Be first out on a Sunday morning to increase your chances even more.

From the junction of CT 167 and CT 10—US 202 in Simsbury—follow CT 167 west .2 mile to Firetown Road and turn right. Proceed down this road for .7 mile and then fork left onto Great Pond Road. The dirt entrance to Great Pond State Forest is on the right in 1.6 mile. After passing an outdoor chapel, frequently used for weddings, the road ends at a parking lot.

We owe the preservation of this 280-acre state forest to James L. Goodwin, the forester and conservationist who established a tree nursery here in 1932. Twenty-four years later, the nursery was designated Connecticut Tree Farm Number One. The land was subsequently bequeathed to the state by Mr. Goodwin and was dedicated as a state forest in 1967.

Many unmarked trails crisscross by the parking lot. This hike starts at the far right corner of the lot and continues in the same direction as the entrance road. This wide (it was an old tote road), well-worn, horseshoe-pocked trail at first goes along the edge of the thick white pine grove and then passes through it. The pines in this planted grove are so dense that no new ones have sprouted despite the millions of seeds shed by opening cones. Instead, the main understory tree is the shade tolerant hemlock. In early summer, pink ladyslippers add color to the soft carpet of pine needles.

Walk past a trail that leaves on the right and then turn right at the next junction onto a woods road that crosses the trail. The pond is visible through the trees. From now on continue to keep the pond at right and follow the trail that circles it. Following this rule of thumb, you may take an occasional dead end to the water's edge—never mind, for these inadvertent side trips permit you to admire the pond from many viewpoints. Shortly after a single bench at the water's edge go right on the trail and onto the boardwalk.

Shallow Great Pond is strewn with lily pads and bordered with emergent vegetation and tree stumps gnawed by beavers. The moisture-loving royal fern stands on water-girt hummocks and even grows in shallow water. Dragonflies dance around and alight with their four wings outspread. Iridescent damselflies flap awkwardly and then perch with wings clasped together above a long thin abdomen. From numerous spots around the pond you can see pine-dotted islands rising from the pond's northern end—we noted that many pines have died in the last few years, probably from drowned roots.

In fall especially, the fallen pine needles on these tote roads create an interesting pattern. If it has been dry of late, a nice fluffy carpet of freshly fallen needles covers the road. If there have been heavy rains the fallen needles outline the flow of the runoff water. Where the water has pooled an even layer of flattened needles tells the story.

Needles falling? But aren't pines evergreens? Yes to both questions. A needle grows in the spring, stays on the tree the first winter (creating the evergreen effect), and is joined the next spring by a crop of fresh new needles. Finally, about one and one-half years after emerging, the needles die and fall. If you walk through a pine grove in early October every little puff of air causes the golden brown needles to drift down to the forest floor.

As your path enters more swampy areas watch for the tupelo (or black gum) tree. Found from Maine to northern Florida, it has an exceptionally wide range but is only found growing naturally in swampy areas. Tupelo has glossy, leathery leaves, slightly teardrop in shape, and deeply furrowed, cross-checked bark, so that it is sometimes referred to as alligator-like. As the leaves change color in the fall this tree presents a deep burgundy red. A good-sized tree (one or two feet in diameter with a record of five feet), it is unfit for most uses. It rots easily and its fibers are so intertwined that it is impossible to split. This tree is fairly common on the borders of the pond.

Just past a stand of the great rhododendron—a native relative of our mountain laurel—bear right around the pond. Come back in mid-July and look for its great white flowers.

About one-quarter of the way around the pond you reach a small boardwalk which carries you over the wetter areas. A little farther on there is another stretch of boardwalk. Often in spring and after prolonged heavy rains, this area is unfortunately under water. In a dry season these sections of boardwalk provide a dry-shod close-up of the lush swamp vegetation.

In this area we froze at the sight of a large doe feeding in a clearing. Moving only when she lowered her head to feed

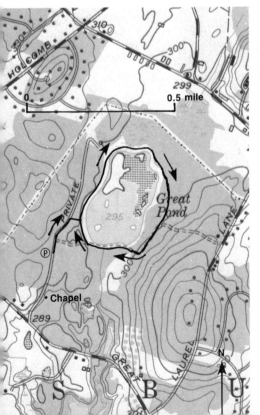

Great Pond through the trees

and freezing during her periodic surveillances, we came within thirty yards of her before our suspicious forms elicited a steady stare. Mosquitos feeding happily on our unmoving forms finally forced us to push on. Her instant flight was punctuated by the highly visible flag of her upraised tail.

Soon cross the bridge at the small cement dam on the south end of the pond. Notice the beaver lodge and evidence of activity just past the dam. Shortly you come to a junction where you may bear left to the parking lot or continue right to the wood benches at the pond's edge. If you choose to sit awhile, you then go left from the benches to the main trail and left again to the parking lot and your car.

3

Larsen Sanctuary

Total Distance: 1.5 miles
Time: ¾ hour
Rating: D
Highlights: Farm Pond, nature center
Map: USGS 7½' Westport

Save this walk for a lazy summer day. An oasis in the urban sprawl of Fairfield County, Larsen Sanctuary is small, and its 6.5 mile trail network traverses flat, undemanding terrain. While it lacks the rolling hills and sweeping vistas of many Connecticut trails, intriguing names like Cottontail Cutoff, Dirty Swamp Trail, and Old Farm Trail hint at the diverse habitats to be discovered. Because of the predominance of low, marshy land so attractive to birds, the sanctuary makes a particularly fine birding area.

To reach the sanctuary from the eastbound lanes of the Merritt Parkway (CT 15), take exit 44 in Fairfield and immediately turn right (west). From the westbound lanes, take exit 45, and at the end of the exit go left, pass under the parkway, and immediately turn right. Either way you are on Congress Street, which you follow for 1.2 miles to Burr Street. Turn right and drive 1.1 miles to the sanctuary entrance on your left.

Larsen Sanctuary is owned and run by the Connecticut Audubon Society. Admission is charged to go on the trails. There is no charge, however, for Fairfield residents or members of the Connecticut Audubon Society.

A massive contemporary gray building houses the nature center, which in addition to the usual bookstore and exhibit areas has a large auditorium and library. Both the studious nature lover and the casual browser can spend many a worthwhile hour here. The nature center is closed on Mondays, but you may still hike the trails.

You approach the trail system through a small structure reminiscent of a covered bridge, to the right of the nature center. Pick up a trail map on the way through. From the multitude of paths we chose a route that hits several points of interest. Although it was early March when we first explored this sanctuary, it was alive with birds. A trio of ducks flew overhead and several other species sang from the trees and underbrush. We heard the distinctive flutter and owl-like moan of the mourning dove and the cheerful (though far from melodious) cry of that faithful harbinger of spring, the red-winged blackbird.

The trail at the start, strewn with wood chips, heads left through scattered overgrown apple trees past the Trail for the Disabled (on the right). Mountain laurel and rhododendron flank that trail, while a pair of open fences guide the way.

Shortly, go right on Garden Marsh Trail, cross a bridge, and bear right at the fork on Old Farm Trail. As you pass Garden Marsh Pond, almost hidden on the left, note the wood duck nesting boxes set on poles above the water. Sweet-scented honeysuckle vines festoon many trees along the marshy pond's edge, and heavy growth of sharp, spiny greenbriar vines guard both sides of the trail.

At the next fork bear right (a left turn takes you on the circuit around Garden Marsh). Shortly you pass through a little clearing. Here a trailing vine of the blackberry family, the dewberry, winds around the tall grasses. The rather sour edible black berries can be refreshing on a hot humid day.

Continue on the Old Farm Trail past the Azalea Trail (left), Deer Meadow Trail (right), and Seep Trail (left) before reaching Pin Oak Swamp Trail. The trail signs

are high overhead on trees. Turn right here through an opening in a stone wall. Notice how the maple tree on your right has grown over the wire that was once nailed to its surface. Deeply buried metal objects such as this have damaged the equipment of many an unsuspecting sawyer!

Much of the trail is slightly elevated on pairs of planks attached to supporting railroad ties or other heavy cross pieces. This not only keeps your feet dry but, more importantly, protects the trail. If it were not so elevated the thousands of tramping feet would make a quagmire of the trail. Future users would edge to one side or the other to avoid the swampy mess and would only widen it.

Proceed past the unsigned Cottontail Cutoff (left). The trail soon runs the length of a low earthfill dam. The shallow marshy pond behind it (to your right) is an ideal wildlife habitat.

Bear left at the next two junctions, fol-

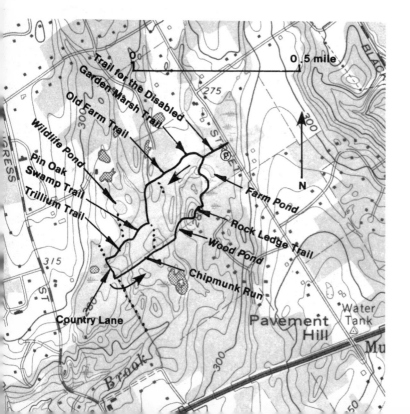

At the entrance to Larsen Sanctuary trails

lowing Trilium Trail and then Country Lane. Just after the wire barrier (to stop horses) leave Country Lane and go left again onto Chipmunk Run, which is an old town road. You now begin the loop back toward the nature center.

In earlier days, the stone walls on either side separated farmer's fields from passers-by. A route flanked on both sides by stone walls is almost surely a town road. Pass, successively, Muskrat Hollow Trail (right) and Cottontail Cutoff (left). Stay on Chipmunk Run; a Tennessee Natural Gas pipeline parallels our trail. A short distance past the end of Old Farm Trail (left), the trail forks at the top of a small rise. Azalea Trail goes left; stay right on Chipmunk Run. As you descend, railroad ties set into the hillside provide secure footing.

Just before crossing the brook below Wood Pond on a substantial wooden bridge, go left to Bench #3 and explore the cavelike rock ledge above. Little children love this sort of place. Cross

the bridge and immediately go right on Rock Ledge Trail (Streamside Trail goes left). Bear left at the top of the rise and follow the twists and turns of Rock Ledge Trail. Shortly after the two paths rejoin, you reach Farm Pond, which has large numbers of tame mallard ducks and Canada geese — a good place to dispose of leftover bread. If you have none, there are two food dispensers where you may purchase seeds to feed the ducks for a quarter. The pond has a wire fence around it to keep its inhabitants from wandering. All have malformed wings or other problems that keep them from flying.

At the junction, go right and continue past Garden Marsh Trail (left) to the entrance. Before leaving the sanctuary, visit the compound for injured animals behind the center. Here, with a special permit from the state, the Connecticut Audubon Society treats more than 500 injured animals each year. Most are eventually returned to the wild.

Mount Tom Tower

Total Distance: 1.5 miles
Time: 1 hour
Rating: C
Highlights: Tower views, state park
Maps: USGS 7½′ New Preston, Mount Tom State Park map

Though short, this is a rewarding half-day hike. By using the swimming and picnicking facilities, you can profitably spend the whole day. The tree-topping tower on the crest of the mountain offers a full 360-degree view of the surrounding countryside.

Mount Tom State Park is located just off US 202 southwest of Litchfield, .6 mile east of its junction with CT 341. Watch for the state park sign by the access road (Old Town Road). Once inside the 233-acre park (a fee is charged on most summer days), follow the one-way signs to a junction with a sign that directs you right to the Tower Trail. Park in the picnic area.

Take the white-blazed trail straight up a steep gravel road (no vehicles allowed). Silver birch and red oak predominate on this slope. In early spring you will see the white blossoms of the shadbush (or Juneberry), so named because it flowers about the time the shad run up the rivers. This shrub, with its light grey bark, is much less noticeable at other times of the year. The juicy berries which ripen in June are edible and taste not unlike huckleberries. The Native Americans used to dry and compress them into great loaves, chunks of which were broken off over the winter for use as a sweetener.

In about ¾ mile the trail ends at the base of a circular stone tower 34 feet high. Wooden stairs inside lead you to a cement roof—watch your head as you emerge. You may see turkey buzzards soaring on Mt. Tom's thermals.

Below is spring-fed Mt. Tom Pond with its bathhouses and trucked-in sand beaches. Beyond Mt. Tom Pond to the northwest you see the Riga plateau with (from left to right) Mounts Bear (see Hike 40), Race, and Everett (the latter pair of mountains are in Massachusetts). To the right of the plateau and beyond Bantam Lake, a popular boating and fishing spot, white church spires mark the historic town of Litchfield. Toward the southwest the rugged hills contain New York's Harriman Park. On very clear days you can see Long Island Sound to the south with the outskirts of New York City at right.

To return by a different route, follow the white blazes back down, but at the

Stone chimney on Mount Tom

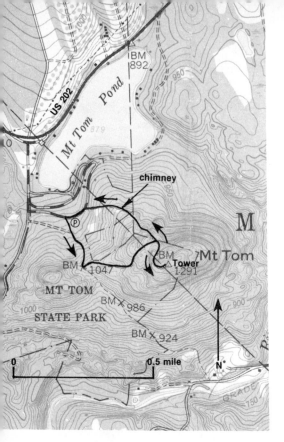

gravel road to the left until it turns left; now take the path that branches right downhill. Log steps embedded in the slope reduce the erosion caused by the straight downhill route. Go left at the tar road and in about 1/10 mile you will see the path marked Tower Trail that you started on.

In mid-April we encountered our first black flies of the season here. Three biting insects are dominant in Connecticut: black flies, mosquitos, and deer flies. Black flies need well-oxygenated running water to breed in, so their season is mercifully short here (further north they are a longer-term merciless scourge). Only repellents that contain high percentages of DEET work against them. Mosquitos breed in stagnant water, but good repellents work. In later spring deer flies arrive, hovering around your head and waiting for a chance to land and dig in. Fortunately they rarely occur in great numbers, so by paying attention you can usually kill them as they alight and reduce your personal cloud of these pests with great satisfaction.

As we stood by the car discussing the hike, a pileated woodpecker, red-crested with white underwings, flew overhead. This uncommon bird, as large as a crow, is the drummer that excavates great rectangular holes in unsound trees to reach infestations of carpenter ants.

first level spot turn right at the grassy area down a steep, rocky, white-blazed trail. You should have no problem following the well-worn treadway.

Near the bottom, as you approach a gravel road, you pass a handsome stone chimney and fireplace with nearby cement foundations. Unfortunately their origin is unknown to us. Follow the

5

Gillette Castle

Total Distance: 2 miles
Time: 1¼ hours
Rating: CD
Highlights: River views, castle
Maps: USGS 7½' Deep River, state park map

Most hikes in this book take you into areas where the pedestrian attractions far exceed those that you can see from your car. Gillette Castle is an exception. A visit to this eccentric structure provides a grand excuse to explore by road the picturesque Haddam-Lyme countryside and to indulge in a short ferry ride. The two state-operated ferries across the Connecticut River harken back to the days of a more leisurely pace and are a fit transition to this area with its turn-of-the-century aura.

If you are starting somewhere west of the Connecticut River, come over on the Chester-Hadlyme ferry (CT 148), which offloads a few miles from the castle, and return on the South Glastonbury-Rocky Hill run about 25 miles north on CT 160. (Both ferries cross at regular intervals during the warmer months and charge a nominal fee.) From the Chester-Hadlyme Ferry continue east on CT 148 to River Road on the left. If you are starting east of the river, take CT 148 west out of Hadlyme and turn right onto River Road (from this direction you must plan a detour to accommodate ferry crossings). Follow the signs on River Road to Gillette Castle (on the left); the parking

area is about .6 mile west from the entrance. On your way in, notice Castle Oak, a giant white oak with a girth of 14 feet. More signs direct you from the parking area to the castle.

This eccentric edifice was built between 1914 and 1919 by William Gillette, one of the most popular figures of the American stage. Acclaimed for his portrayal of Sherlock Holmes, Gillette was born and bred in Connecticut; he lived in the castle until his death in 1937. Unbelievable though it seems, the interior of this building nearly outdoes the exterior. Granite walls, hand-hewn interior oak trim, built-in furniture, intricate wooden locks, and unique light fixtures are only some of its attractions. The "castle" is open daily from Memorial Day to Columbus Day. Admission is charged.

After exploring the castle's wonders and perhaps lunching at an adjacent picnic table, walk the few yards north of the castle to "Grand Central Station," the main terminal for the now dismantled Seventh Sister Shortline. This three mile-long miniature railroad was Gillette's pride and joy. He often treated his guests to a ride while he manned the throttle. The park's trail system crosses, parallels, and follows this old miniature railroad bed. As you walk along this old railroad bed imagine William Gillette delightedly piloting the train around the curves and by the rock walls while his passengers look on with amazement (or possibly some other emotion).

Pass through the station toward the river and follow the flagstone ramp (right) down to the sign that reads, "Loop Trail to River Vista, 0.5 mile" and bear left along a fence. You wind down through thick young hemlocks interspersed with black birch. Bear left and please stay on the trail; too much unneeded erosion has been caused by shortcuts down the fragile slope. The switchbacks in the area are designed to allow the maximum amount of use with the minimum amount of damage.

As you walk, look sharply through the gaps in the trees for excellent views of the Connecticut River. Where you first start on this trail along the fence there is an excellent cameo view of the ferry! Af-ter about .25 mile, the trail circles back along the face of a wall, crosses an attractive covered footbridge which you bypassed at the start of the loop, and rejoins the outward branch. (The covering over wooden bridges wasn't for romantic purposes, but shielded the wooden roadbed from the elements).

Return to the "Loop Trail" sign and bear left along the upper trail. Go right up to an ornate stone and cement gate that leads to an equally ornate "outhouse." A short piece of the original track has been preserved here. Retrace your steps to the trail and go right. The trail soon parallels and lies below the tar road that you followed in to the castle's parking lot. At your first junction, continue straight ahead; bear left at the next junction, and then right.

Descend the wooden steps on your left. The Connecticut River is often glimpsed through the hemlocks at left. After tending downward a good ways the trail levels off and then starts to climb by a piped spring. A few yards

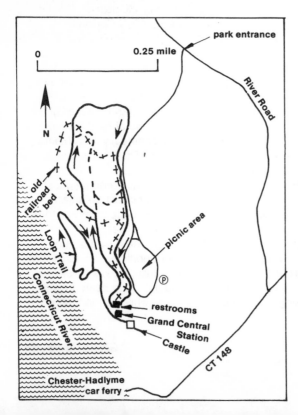

Gillette Castle

beyond the spring there is a black birch (left) with a large amount of rotting heartwood. The rounded living edges show that the tree is trying to span this fungus-admitting gap with living tissue.

Shortly after you start upward the trail describes a sharp right. After your right turn, continue uphill until you reach the old railroad bed again, then go right. A little further on, just after you pass the wooden steps you went down earlier, you reach a fork—go left. Soon, at the next junction just before the tar road, you go right. The railroad bed is seen below at your right. At the next junction, go left. You pass through rock cuts carved for the miniature railroad. Occasionally you will pass rotting remnants of the original railroad ties and ceramic pipes which helped keep the railroad bed drained. Pass over two wooden bridges with the ever-present tar entrance road on your left. You soon come to the castle; bear left to your car in the parking lot.

During this walk you may have noticed viny vegetation with single leaves. This was probably Oriental bittersweet— an alien that has a propensity to choke trees and bushes.

Greenwich Audubon Sanctuary

Total Distance: 2.5 miles
Time: 1½ hours
Rating: C
Highlights: Nature Center, rich mature hardwood forest
Map: USGS 7½' Glenville

Mention Greenwich, and you may invoke visions of high-walled estates surrounded by dense urban areas and ribbons of concrete. Long ago urban New York City engulfed this southwest corner of Connecticut. A visit to the 280-acre Greenwich Audubon Sanctuary is a pleasant surprise; its woodland beauty compares favorably with many wilder, less accessible areas of the state. Rolling hills, large hardwoods on rich bottomland soil, swamps, a small river, and a pond attract many kinds of birds, including the pale-faced city-jaded hiker.

To reach the sanctuary, take exit 28 from the Merritt Parkway (CT 15) and turn north (right) onto Round Hill Road. After 1.5 miles, turn left onto John Street. Drive for 1.4 miles to Riverville Road; the Audubon Center entrance and parking lot are on your right. In addition to maintaining a network of easy trails, the Center, which is open Tuesday through Sunday from 9 AM to 5 PM, operates an excellent bookstore, an interpretive center with seasonal exhibits, and a variety of natural history programs and demonstrations on weekends. All are worth the nominal entrance fee (no charge for National Audubon Society members).

Before you begin walking, pick up a map of the trail system at the Center. There are no painted blazes here to help you but there are signs at all the trail junctions. As you can see from the map there are many trails here to explore—we describe one loop—and you may want to try some or all of the others.

Starting by a large sign showing the trail system in contrasting colors, follow the paved Orchard Hill Road left downhill, through an orchard dotted with birdhouses. A bit beyond where you turn left there is an apple tree with several rows of evenly spaced holes in the bark. These holes are unmistakably the work of a provident woodpecker with the unglamorous name of yellow-bellied sapsucker. He drills the neat rows one day and returns on succeeding days to drink the sap that has welled up in the holes and to feast on insects that have been attracted by the free lunch. After examining this tree, go back a few yards and head down the grass-bordered lane labeled "Discovery Trail, Lake Mead," now a left turn.

In a short distance, the trail becomes surrounded by thick undergrowth, especially blackberry canes with their rank growth and formidable thorns. The trail tends downhill. Level log steps partially embedded in and perpendicular to the route of the trail retard the damaging erosion that running water can create as it courses down a trail. Without the steps the well-traveled path would rapidly erode. (The wood chips that you find elsewhere on the trail are not meant to ease your way but to protect the trail.) Most of this sanctuary with its well-grown trees is made up of rich bottom-land hardwoods—beech, ash, tulip trees, oak, and maple. The woods are left to their own natural growth and eventual decay. The Audubon personnel do not "improve" the area. Dying trees and fallen branches are left to rot where they fall, creating a cornucopia of life for the diverse creatures of the sanctuary.

Shortly the Clovis Trail goes off to the right. Continue left on the Discovery Trail down to Byram River, cross the bridge, and proceed uphill. Soon the Discovery Trail bends left, crosses the dam at Lake Mead, and eventually returns to the Audubon center. Do not cross the dam, but keep right uphill on an old tote road called the Riverbottom Road past a patch of greenbriar. The stem of this thorny vine is green year-round; its tangled masses are particularly distinctive during the leafless months.

While traversing these trails in well-heeled suburbia, you may ponder the value of the land in this 280-acre oasis. You might want to think in terms of the Crown Jewels of England. The value of the gems and precious metals they contain are far less than their worth as a whole. So with this very rare oasis—its

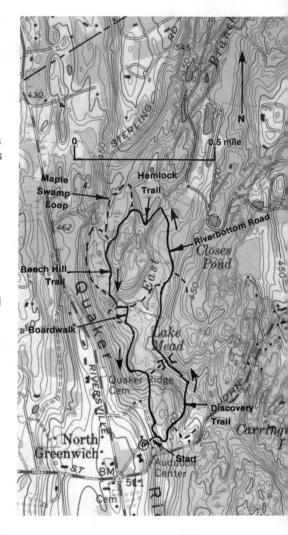

value broken up and sold as lots is far less than its value now and to the future generations that will explore these woods.

The trail now runs atop a low ridge with glimpses of Lake Mead below on your left. Elaborate bird blinds hug the closest shore. You may have noticed a straggly vine clinging to many trees and shrubs along the path. This vine, the

Oriental or Asiatic bittersweet, depends entirely on its coiling ability to work skyward, unlike poison ivy and Virginia creeper, which hoist themselves up with the aid of aerial roots. Because its coils cut deep spiral ridges in host plants, often strangling them, this alien is considered a pest in the sanctuary.

The trail descends gradually, cutting through a stone wall (the Lake Trail leaves on the left), and then climbs gently. Proceed straight on Riverbottom Road and bear left at the next junction. You soon reach the Byram River again.

The muddy flood plain on the far side of the river is liberally dotted with skunk cabbage, a rather unattractive and malodorous plant that blossoms very early in the spring. Its shape and smell are specially adapted to attract the only insects available for pollination this early— carrion flies who search out carcasses of animals who died the previous winter. Attracted by the dark reddish color of the hoodlike spathe and the fetid odor, the flies mistake skunk cabbage flowers for a dead animal. In the process of investigating, the flies pollinate the tiny flowers inside the spathe.

After crossing the river, follow the trail up the slope through a large grove of beech trees. Riverbottom Road terminates at the top of this rise. Proceed left on Hemlock Trail. This route is neither blazed nor well-worn so be careful following it. Be particularly alert because the trail zigzags sharply to the right.

The Hemlock Trail skirts a swamp on the right, then rises sharply to its junction with Maple Swamp Trail. Turn left. Note the boundary marker near the junction of these trails—a large pile of stones resting on a glacial boulder.

The Maple Swamp Trail climbs steadily to the Beech Hill Trail—again bear left. This trail drops gradually and merges with Hillside Trail which you also follow to the left.

You pass more large beeches here. Unfortunately, defacing initials carved on the smooth, tender bark can still be easily deciphered after the passage of many years.

At a fork go left. You are now on the Lake Trail. Soon a right turn takes you out onto a boardwalk built in 1977. The amount and variety of species growing in this swampy area are truly amazing. Soon you reach the west side of Lake Mead. Continue on the Lake Trail to its junction with the Discovery Trail; go right to Orchard Road. Look right for an old root cellar embedded in the hillside before turning left for a short walk back to your car.

Skunk cabbage leaves and spathe in spring

7

Hurd State Park

Total Distance: 2.5 miles
Time: 1½ hours
Rating: CD
Highlight: Connecticut River view
Map: USGS 7½' Middle Haddam

Serendipity. It's a lovely sounding word with a beautiful meaning: "the faculty of making fortunate and unexpected discoveries by accident." Perhaps the most famous example of serendipity was Sir Alexander Fleming's discovery of penicillin while investigating the noxious green mold that was killing his bacteria cultures. For a hiker, serendipity should be a familiar byword. In this book we point out what we have seen, but you should always be prepared for serendipitous happenings. Remember that "adventure is not in the guidebook and beauty is not on the map."

With this thought in mind, pay a visit to Hurd State Park, perched on the east bank of the Connecticut River. From the junction of CT 151 and CT 66 in Cobalt, drive south on CT 151 for 2.4 miles and bear right at the Hurd State Park sign. You reach the park entrance on the right in .5 mile. Another right turn about .5 mile down this tar road at the "Shelter/Ballfield" leads to a delightful rainy-day picnic shelter with two great stone fireplaces and tables galore. To reach the hiking trails drive past this access road to the "Trail" sign at left 1.1 mile from the park entrance. There is ample parking here on the right.

As we entered the park on a recent visit, we saw a bluebird, the first we'd spotted in a few years. Bluebirds are the same shade as the most breathtaking patch of sky you've ever seen. Unfortunately their numbers have dropped because of competition with a pair of drab aliens—the English sparrow and the starling. A few people are trying to redress the balance by constructing bluebird trails with a series of just-so bird houses along forest margins. With luck and the effort of these dedicated people, this rare sight might again become common.

Follow the trail (yellow blazes) left onto an old tote road and then to a well-trodden path. (The River Trail connects here, but save it for later.)

Walking along here early one morning, we froze at a movement farther down the trail. A spotted fawn tottered to an uncertain stop, eyed us a bit, snorted to absorb our smell better, and—deciding that we were dubious characters—bounded back down the trail. Serendipity!

After ¼ mile or so of gentle climbing, leave the trail at the sign and walk out onto a white rock ledge for the River Vista. Across the river to the left is Bear Hill (see Hike 42, Seven Falls). Only power lines—progress—mar this view of the hills along the river.

Go back to the sign and head downhill past a great white glacial boulder. Follow the trail down to the Split Rock sign and go left to more river views and Split Rock itself, a narrow crevasse twenty-five feet deep. Retrace your steps and climb back uphill parallel to the ledge. Rejoin the trail and retrace your steps almost to the beginning.

Now take the River Trail (pink or faded red) which proceeds leisurely downhill through ferns and other undergrowth to a large grassy picnic area near the river. This grassy area is used mostly by boaters plying the river. Across the river to the right is the United Technologies jet engine facility. In addition to private craft, tugs pushing rusty barges occasionally chug by.

Spend a while exploring the riverside. Wandering off to the left we saw two young black ducks in a quiet spot. The trees here are different from those on the surrounding hillsides: sycamores, dying elms, tall sassafras, cottonwoods, silver maples, and willow form this forest canopy. The open areas, covered with coarse grass glistening with dew on clear summer mornings, are fringed with bouncing bet and podded milkweeds. Retrace your steps and continue right along the riverbank and across the small stream—note the path and two

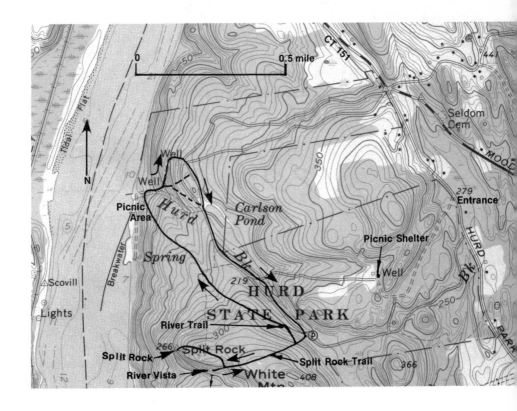

Tugboat and barge on the Connecticut River

tote roads to the right. After exploring the northern end of the riverside's grassy area, head uphill on any of these three trails—they all join shortly.

There is a hand pump where the three trails meet; you might want to stop for a cooling drink of water. Continue steadily uphill, keeping the brook ravine on your right. At the next fork, bear left and then curve slowly right with the trail until you emerge on the tar park loop road (green blazes). Here there is a wooden trail map. Turning right you soon pass a rock wall on your right which was built by the Civilian Conservation Corps (CCC) in the 1930s. You see a frog pond on your left before reaching your car.

Highland Springs and Lookout Mountain

Total Distance: 2.5 miles
Time: 1½ hours
Rating: C
Highlights: Hemlock grove, views
Map: USGS 7½' Rockville

Billed as the "Purest and Best Table Water in the World," bottled mineral water from the springs at Highland Park was once distributed throughout southern New England and as far away as New Jersey. However, while the water bottling business is now flourishing as it did in the nineteenth century, this particular spring has been sealed off. The pollution that closed the spring may have come from the numerous housing developments that have sprung up in the area in recent years.

The loop trail begins at the Highland Springs parking lot. From eastbound I-384 in Manchester, take exit 4, Wyllys Street. From the end of the exit ramp, go right on Wyllys Street about .2 miles to the small parking lot at the bottom of the hill on the left. From westbound I-384, take exit 4, Highland Street; go right at the end of the exit ramp to the traffic light. This is Wyllys Street; turn right, cross over the highway, and proceed as above. The town bought this area under the now obsolete open-space program.

Before starting out, look for the large piebald barked sycamore standing near the trail head. The piebald effect results

from the tree's normal growth; while the bark of most growing trees splits into vertical furrows as new wood forms just inside, the sycamore's bark periodically breaks off in plates, leaving a clean white surface which contrasts markedly with the older, darker bark.

From the parking lot, follow the paved road to Lookout Mountain uphill into a thick stand of hemlocks, keeping the chain-link fence on your left. Old light blue blazes crossed with horizontal yellow paint bars mark your way. Soon the road becomes a wide gravel path. Turn right into the woods on an unmarked trail in sight of new homes and a paved cul-de-sac. Shortly you reach the old deeply eroded trail; turn left uphill. The path is well-worn but poorly marked.

In about three-quarters of a mile you cross an old gravel road that goes directly to the lookout. If you had continued on the gravel path, you would have run into this road. The hemlock begins to thin out until it is almost wholly replaced with oak and a scattering of maple, hickory, and black birch. The soil here may look the same to us but the thirsty roots of the hemlock know the difference.

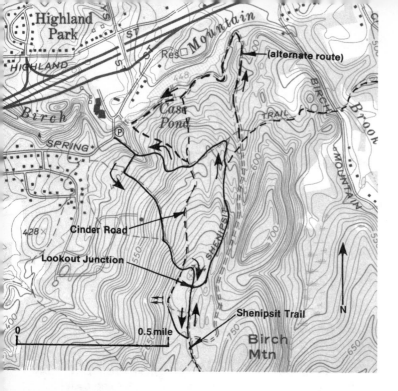

After another ¼ mile you come to a trail crossing known as Lookout Junction. The blue and yellow blazes go right, but you should continue straight ahead onto the blue-blazed Shenipsit Trail, which leads to Gay City State Park (see Hike 23) some six miles to the south. Today you will only follow the blue blazes a short distance past a screen of laurel to a thirty-foot high hemlock on your right. Look to the right—there is a mysterious clearing where only sedges and mosses grow. Surrounding the opening are numerous highbush blueberry plants that are heavily laden in season. Unfortunately these berries, though beautiful, are extremely sour—perhaps because of a very acidic soil. No woody plants grow within the opening; it is possible that the annual spring snow melt flooding kills them.

Retrace your steps to the junction and follow the blue and yellow blazes to the left up a small rise to a gravel clearing, the summit of Lookout Mountain (744 feet). Note carefully where you enter the lookout clearing to ease your way back onto the trail.

The view from the lookout depends upon the visibility; too often, especially in summer, Connecticut Valley smog reduces your horizon. Manchester lies in the foreground but because of its well-treed streets, this city of 60,000 is hard to see. Only the flat, smoke-stacked box of the high school and the white spire of Center Congregational Church are readily identifiable. In the middle distance the towers and high-rise office buildings of Hartford stand out, and on a very clear day you can see the white finger of the Heublein Tower (see Hike 37) rising from Talcot Mountain northwest of Hartford.

Return yet again to the junction and proceed straight across onto the joint Shenipsit Trail/Highland Park loop. The trail curves gently left along the top of a ridge above an old stone quarry. To the right the land drops off quickly in stepped ledges to a flat forest floor. On the left lies a long narrow depression which snow melt floods each spring. At that time of year it serves as a breeding

These black-masked, tan-colored frogs are the earliest spring breeders of our native amphibians. Although probably more numerous than the familiar spring peepers, they lack the high-pitched carrying cry of the latter and are therefore not as well known. You often hear their low croaks in this area as early as the fourth week of March. The tadpoles, though safe from most predators, must go through their metamorphosis and become small frogs quickly, since the depression is dry by summer.

The thin poor soil along the exposed ledges of the ridge dries out quickly and is largely treed with chestnut oaks, which are more tolerant of poor, dry soil than the water-loving hemlocks. With their deep-furrowed dark grey bark, these oaks are distinctive at any season. The trail now slopes down toward the

Trail signs at the junction at the McLean Game Refuge

flat forest floor. After bearing right downhill, near the end of the ridge go left.

Hemlocks are thick about the trail again—a legacy of the moisture from Highland Springs on the other side of the hill. Watch for the turn where the blue blazes bear right downhill. (The blue-blazed Shenipsit Trail drops down and continues reaching Birch Mountain Road in .6 miles.) At this point continue straight ahead on the blue and yellow blazes. Along this ridge the trail is marked with faded blue and blue/yellow blazes, one above the other. Watch carefully for a double blaze and a faded arrow on a large chestnut oak tree to the left of the trail near the end of the ridge. Turn left uphill.

The blazes (faded to almost nothing), blue with a horizontal yellow bar, run only a short distance toward the open mesh fence near the top of the hill. Just before reaching the fence (on your right) you pass a lightning-riven hemlock. Notice the strip of removed wood and bark slashing down one side of the tree. The extreme temperature induced by the lightning vaporized the tree's sap, causing the wood to literally explode.

Although there are few blazes here, continue along and bear right on the old trail that leads to an old road. Go left on the road and at the fork, go left, cross under the bar and rejoin the road you started up on. Go right downhill to your car.

Should you have difficulty following the old trail, retrace your steps to the blue-blazed Shenipsit Trail and follow that downhill to a dirt road. Go left on the dirt road as it wends its way, soon reaching Case Pond. Stay on the old road and in ¼ mile or so, by a stone staircase, go left uphill on a dirt road running between stone walls. Shortly at the fork turn right, go under the bar and rejoin the road you started up on. Go right downhill to your car.

Sat 10/12/98
— Nice time on a gloomy day —
Beautiful foliage on the ride
down Rte. 9!

Rocky Neck

Total Distance: 3 miles
Time: 1½ hours
Rating: D
Highlights: Ocean views, sandy beach, state park
Maps: USGS 7½' Old Lyme, Niantic

Families sometimes have difficulty finding a place everyone will enjoy. The outdoor activities at Rocky Neck State Park are varied enough to provide something for everybody. Youngsters can fish off the jetty, teenagers can loll on the beach, and hikers can explore the practically deserted woodland paths.

The park entrance is located off CT 156, 2.7 miles west of CT 161 in Niantic. If you are traveling on the Connecticut Turnpike (I-95), take exit 72 (Rocky Neck) to CT 156 and follow the signs east (left) to the park. In addition to complete day-use facilities—beach, bathhouses, restrooms, and picnic areas—the park has a separate camping area. The attractive sites scattered amidst trees may be reserved in advance. In summer there is a day-use entry fee. If you are only going to hike you may choose to avoid this fee by parking on CT 156 (about .5 mile east of the park) and starting this loop hike at the log gate there.

Within the park, drive into the first large parking area on the right, 1.6 miles from the entrance (where park maps are available) just beyond the bridge over Brides's Brook. Head for the

far left corner of the lot and the picnic tables; the trail starts at a white blaze on a post to the right of the outhouses. The trail passes quickly through a fringe of oaks and maples to a short causeway leading across a marsh. While crossing the causeway and a small bridge, you are threatened by poison ivy, treated to the sight of large pink swamp roses, startled by ducks you have inadvertently flushed, and delighted by gracefully circling terns.

As you enter the woods beyond the marsh, mountain laurel, sweet pepperbush, blueberries, huckleberries, greenbriar, and sassafras make up the bulk of the thick undergrowth. Several young chestnuts up to thirty feet high are still free of the blight that has ravaged our native chestnuts since shortly after the beginning of the century. The blight's first external sign is small orange-topped fungal bodies that indicate the girdling of the tree and the death of everything above this point. Occasional glacial erratics and rounded ledges complete this scene.

At the junction about a mile from the start, take a short detour straight ahead before continuing. The detour leads to a

Four Mile River and the fogbound bay

field where Japanese honeysuckle, with its highly perfumed yellow or white blossoms, lines the edge. This is the picnic area on CT 156 and alternative starting point, where the trail takes a sharp left on an old road across brackish Four Mile River. Cross Shipyard Field. A boat yard lying across the way reminds you of this hike's shore location. Continue to the junction with the yellow-blazed trail near the top of the hill. Stay on the white trail and bear right at the next two

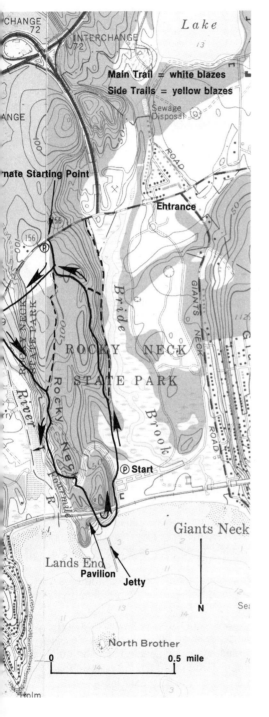

Main Trail = white blazes
Side Trails = yellow blazes

CHANGE
72

INTERCHANGE
72

Lake
13

ANGE

Sewage
Disposal

ROAD

'nate Starting Point

Ehtrance

156

ROCKY NECK
STATE PARK

Bride
Brook

GIANTS NECK

ROAD

P Start

Giants Neck

Lands End
Pavilion
Jetty

N

Se

North Brother

0   0.5 mile

Holm

forks, finally ascending a rocky ridge. Follow the ridge toward the ocean. Views of Four Mile River and the open bay await you, partially obscured at first by oak foliage. Clamshells litter the open ledges. Gulls drop clams from on high and then pick out the meat from the shattered shells.

At the end of the open ridge the trail drops down to the left to meet a path. A right turn soon takes you to a tar road. Proceed to the right through a small parking lot to the paved uphill walkway. This leads you beyond the arched bridge over railroad tracks to an imposing pavilion. A make-work project of the 1930s, the pavilion has given us more than full value! The walls of this massive building are made of fieldstone, and large fireplaces cheer the inside. The internal woodwork includes pillars of great tree trunks; at least one trunk was taken from each then-existing state park.

From the front porch of the pavilion bear left toward a picnic area. A rocky fishing jetty thrusts into the water before you, and beyond it spreads the graceful curve of the beach. The rocky arms at either side of the bay provide shelter from all but the roughest storms.

Turn left through the railroad underpass at the near corner of the beach. Swamp roses adorn the embankment here. If you follow the road straight past the concession stands you will find your car in the second parking lot on the right.

10

11/5/94

Bonnie; "A nice walk in the woods."

Wadsworth Falls

Total Distance: 3 miles
Time: 1¾ hours
Rating: CD
Highlights: Waterfalls, state park, swimming
Map: USGS 7½' Middletown

Moving water has a special fascination for man that is rivaled only by the flickering of fire. The ebb and flow of ocean waves mesmerize us, boiling rapids and cascades captivate our attention, and waterfalls enchant us wherever they occur. This hike features not one but two of these liquid attractions. Best viewed during spring's heavy runoff, the larger of this pair is worth a visit at any season.

From the junction of CT 66 and CT 157 in Middletown take CT 157 southwest following signs to Wadsworth State Park. You will reach the park entrance on the left in 1.6 miles. Since this park has swimming, there is a fee to park here on summer days. In addition to swimming the park features bathhouses, picnic tables, fireplaces and hiking trails.

A nice but not totally reliable carved map of the park's trails has been set up just beyond the entrance. From this spot pass through the picnic grove to the Main Trail which begins by a culverted stream; this trail is blazed with orange paint.

Immediately after crossing a bridge over a small stream that splashes down a series of ledges, the trail forks. Bear right. Cedar, maple, birch, and poplar form the woods backdrop while sweet ferns, yarrow, blackberries, and a large patch of poison ivy line the path. On your left the trail passes one of the largest mountain laurels in the state.

A short distance further on you come to a second small stream. The bridge over this is supported by side walls of masonry cloaked in a patina of mosses and lichens. Here the woods are composed of tall straight hickory, oak, black birch, and hemlock. Red squirrels shout loudly from safe perches far above the trail. Every so often unmarked side trails leave the well-worn main path, inviting exploration.

In ½ mile, when the trail splits, take the right fork toward Little Falls (you will return by the left path). Winding through beautiful treed ravines and slopes (blue blazes), this trail eventually parallels the small stream that glides over the mossy ledges. About ¾ mile from the start you reach Little Falls.

Cross the brook below the falls and climb the steep hill on the right. Be careful as this compacted soil can be slippery when wet. On the hilltop there is a falls overlook to your left.

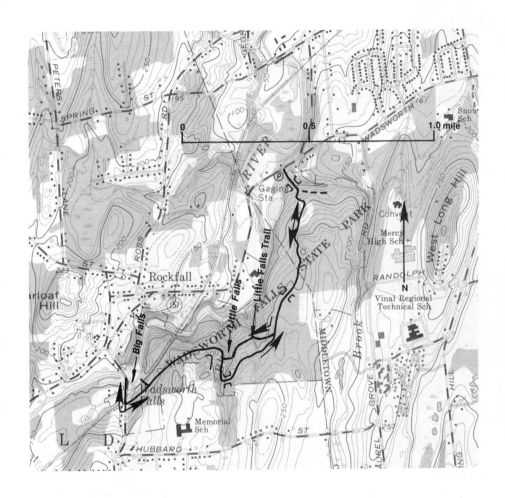

When you have finished admiring the falls, return to the side trail which continues to the nearby wide, worn main trail. Turn right. Less than ¼ mile from the falls and about 1 mile from the start, railroad tracks and power lines appear below on your right. In another ¼ mile you reach the sign to Big Falls.

From here there are two routes to these falls on the Coginchaug River. One is short but the way is steep, and in places, slippery; the other is longer but much safer. Since they both offer

views from opposite sides of the river we suggest you take both.

For the shorter route, turn right down the steep bank to the railroad tracks by several small hemlocks and a large black birch. As you cross the railroad tracks, look around. In summer the bluebells of the creeping bellflower please the eye, and in season black raspberries tickle the palate. Great banks of multiflora roses and a few striking Deptford pinks attract your attention.

Proceed right on the path on the far

Fishermen at Big Falls

side of the tracks. For your first view of Big Falls bear left steeply down an eroded pitch to the brink of the falls. Now head back up a bit, passing through a small stand of handsome twisted beeches, and take the higher and safer of two parallel paths above the pool lying at the base of the falls. To reach the pool, bear off to the right and down a steep slope.

From this vantage point you face the cascading water. Ragged volcanic traprock provides the upper layer of erosion-resistant rock necessary to maintain a waterfall. To the left is a great undercut in the traprock carved by rushing water in ages past.

When you are ready, retrace your steps across the railroad tracks back to the main trail (orange blazes). To view the falls from the other side, take the longer, safer route, which is now on your right. Keep to the main path until you reach a tar road, turn right, cross the railroad tracks, cross the bridge over the river, and descend into a grassy field. Follow the path down to the left. After crossing the edge of a small field you come to the base of the falls. You may have to share this spot with fishermen trying to entice the elusive brown trout. A fenced-in overlook provides yet another view.

To finish this hike, retrace your steps via the tar road to the main trail and follow the orange blazes back to your car.

11

Nayantaquit Trail

Total Distance: 3 miles
Time: 2 hours
Rating: C
Highlights: State forest, plethora of boulders
Map: USGS 7½' Hamburg

People who opt for a fairly constant temperature miss the ebb and flow of the seasons. Connecticut has definite, well-differentiated seasons; each affects what hikers may see; each has something to recommend it. The short period after winter's snow has disappeared but before the spring flowers blossom—usually during the month of March and sometimes in early April—is the perfect time for an "evergreen walk." Except for a few twigs like greenbriar and sassafras (both seen on this hike), everything green is an evergreen—a plant whose foliage is green all year round.

While an "evergreen walk" can be enjoyed in any of our woodland areas, we chose to do ours on the Nayantaquit Trail in Nehantic State Forest in Old Lyme. Some types of evergreens such as lichens, mosses, sedges, and grasses require a specialist's knowledge so we have treated these rather perfunctorily. The evergreens that we saw are noted in the text in parentheses approximately where we found them.

The Nayantaquit Trail, laid out and cut by our good friends Jack and Vel Randall, was opened in April of 1983. It is now a well-defined and very well-marked trail. When we first hiked the Nayantaquit trail it needed footsteps to make it "real." Now it's a delightful loop well cared for by its maintainer, Jim Wheeler.

From the junction of US 1 and CT 156 (exit 70 off I-95N) follow CT 156 north for 7 miles. Go right (east) on Beaver Brook Road and after 2 miles go right on Keeny Road (no sign). Follow Keeny Road for 1 mile where it turns to dirt; in another .3 mile you will see a parking lot on your right.

The trail goes southeast from the parking lot and is marked with blue blazes. A woods road goes northeast from the lot and can easily be used in combination with the trail to lengthen the hike to about 7.5 miles. For example, you could start at the dirt road at the parking lot and go all the way around to the Uncas Pond Trail, go left to the junction with the Loop Trails and follow the North Loop back to your car. Be careful following the blazes, as State Forest personnel have been marking some of the trees for cutting—using, among other colors, blue! Follow the trail up a small hill (tree club moss, running ground pine, cushion moss, hair-

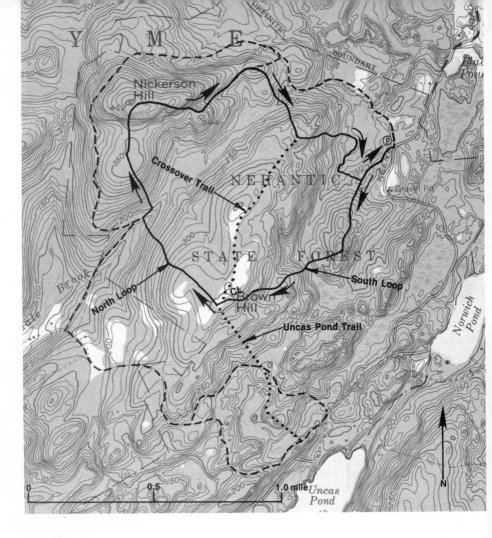

cap moss, reindeer moss, polypody fern). Note that several families of plants are called "moss" but not all are mosses—reindeer moss is a lichen and the eight varieties of club moss which appear around do not belong in the moss family, either.

Continue over a rocky knoll (Christmas fern, evergreen wood fern, red spruce) to the well-signed junction. Follow the South Loop left (spotted wintergreen) soon crossing an old tote road and a stone wall and climb a gentle rise. Stone walls are everywhere here; they separated fields before the settlers died off,

moved to the cities, and/or went west to find rock-free fertile soil. Rounding the hilltop, the trail bears slightly right (southeast) at the double blazes.

Entering a rock-strewn area, the trail again goes right—notice the rock tripe (a lichen) on some of the boulders as you climb the next small hill (cinquefoil).

Cross a small stream (staghorn club moss) and continue up the rock-studded hill. The trail curves right and crosses another brook, chockfull of algae. As you start the last steep grade up Brown Hill look at the large straight tulip tree (about 3' in diameter) to your left (dewberry). As you reach the open rock ledge you will pass a sizeable red cedar (another evergreen) and a cherry tree struggling for existence in a mass of rock. Cherry trees almost always have twigs misshapen with thick black masses of black knot fungus—watch for this on cherries when the leaves are off. Crossing another stone wall, you reach an old hilltop meadow where the trail signs decorate a beautifully formed white oak. Take time to explore and enjoy the area. To the north there are remnants of an old stone shelter. Small trees grow as the forest begins to claim the once cleared field.

Take the left trail to Nickerson Hill. (The right trail or "crossover" divides the Nayantaquit Trail into north and south loops.) Shortly cross Uncas Pond Trail, but stay on the loop trail which veers right and then left downhill on an old tote road. Watch closely lest you be lulled by the downhill rhythm of your walk and miss the sharp right turn that the trail makes off the road. At the bottom of the hill again join an old road, cross the brook and head right uphill with the blue blazes on still another old road. Soon the blazes fork left away from the road. The trail levels a bit and then climbs directly up Nickerson Hill. Glacial erratics are everywhere around you. Reaching the top of the hill, cross the stone wall and immediately go right as the trail ambles downhill.

Cross a stone wall and climb slightly to reach another junction. Here we followed the loop trail bearing right. If you continue straight ahead to the woods road, a right on the road will take you back to your car. Staying on the loop trail, you soon cross a gurgling brook. Continue uphill (rattlesnake plantain) to

Trail signs at the hilltop meadow

the junction with the crossover trail to Brown Hill. Our trail leads to the parking area through a break in a stone wall then downhill. Cross a grassy swath and go right, soon crossing a small brook and proceeding through a swampy area. Then bear left across another grassy swath and return to the junction where you started the loop. Continue left to your car.

12

Pine Knob Loop

Total Distance: 2.5 miles
Time: 1¾ hours
Rating: A
Highlight: Views
Map: USGS 7½' Ellsworth

Located on the edge of the Housatonic River Valley in western Connecticut, the double peaks of Pine Knob command excellent views of this beautiful river. In contrast to the large and rather dirty Connecticut River, the Housatonic here is a cozy little river winding down a scenic valley—its upper reaches are still relatively clean.

To reach this hike's start, drive to the western end of Cornwall Bridge (near the junction of US 4 and US 7) and head north on US 7 for a mile. A blue oval sign proclaims "Pine Knob Loop." Although there is a parking area off the road you may have to compete with trout fishermen for a parking space—the Housatonic here is perhaps the premier trout river in the state.

The blue-blazed trail starts at a tote road on the north end of the parking area; a triple blaze on a maple tree marks the start of the trail. Old house foundations and a pleasant crossing of Hatch Brook meet your eye immediately. This section of trail cuts through mixed woods of oak, ash, maple, and hickory with a few crinkly-barked black cherry trees scattered throughout. Shortly the trail enters a planted white

pine grove. The five-leaved vine climbing many of these pines is Virginia creeper; the leaves of this harmless vine turn flaming crimson in the fall.

In .2 mile, you reach a trail junction. Continue straight on the North Loop which parallels US 7 on your right. You will come to a second junction in another .2 mile—here fork left. (The right fork leads you to the campground at Housatonic Meadows State Park.) As you ascend the steep hill, stubby oaks predominate on the thin, well-drained soil between ledge outcroppings.

Just beyond where the trail levels a bit, several chestnut saplings grow. Once considered to be one of North America's most important hardwoods—valued both for its extremely durable wood and for its nuts—the chestnut has fallen prey to a deadly fungal blight. First noticed in New York's Botanical Gardens in 1904, the bark-girdling fungus spread quickly, almost eliminating the tree. The loss of the chestnut was one of our greatest natural calamities. Despite major efforts at Yale and elsewhere, no sure solution to the disease has yet been discovered. Since the tree only dies from the girdled spot up

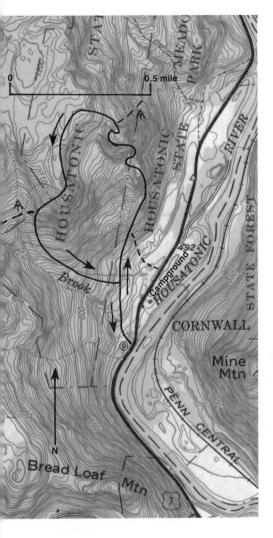

peak of Pine Knob is visible on the extreme right. At left center on one of the rounded peaks well beyond the river, you can see Mohawk Mountain's distinctive towers against the horizon. The seemingly endless rounded hills swimming across your vision help explain why northwestern Connecticut is the most popular area for hiking within the state.

A few years ago while hiking here in the rain with Bob Redington, who laid out Pine Knob Loop, we met an Appalachian Trail (AT) "through hiker." This driven breed of hiker feels the need to hike all the 2,025 miles of this linear National Park in a single season. The young man we met had started in Georgia and was moved to distraction by all the road walking he had endured in New York. He was wandering over these ridges—in 1977, far from the AT—to avoid Connecticut's road sections! (Such road walking, which private landowners increasingly insist on, is one of the reasons why the National Park Service has almost completed acquiring a permanent right-of-way for the AT).

The trail turns right off the overlook and passes over the top of this viewless wooded first knob (1,120 feet), before dropping down steeply to the col between the two peaks. In another .5 mile on the far side of the second knob (1,160 feet), you come to another lookout. Stop and relax—perhaps you will see a pair of red-tailed hawks gracefully circling the valley as we did!

Continuing off this second knob, the trail now (in 1990) joins the Appalachian Trail and drops steeply while the sound of unseen flowing water gradually invades your subconscious. Today the AT in Connecticut is nearly entirely protected and it has been relocated to the western side of the Housatonic River.

and sprouts readily from its roots, the chestnut remains a common small tree.

In another .3 mile a viewpoint reveals a state campground almost directly before you nestled among the trees across US Route 7. Circling left, the trail starts its final ascent of the first knob over displaced, tumbled ledges. After another .3 mile the trail continues left along a rocky terrace. As you face the river, the other

Housatonic Meadows Campground from the North Loop

Pine Knob Loop and the AT run together for nearly three quarters of a mile. In a small hemlock grove about .3 mile from the last lookout watch for a blue arrow directing you sharply left. The depression containing Hatch Brook is visible on your right between two glacial erratics. Here too is where we leave the AT as its white blazes continue south to Springer Mountain in Georgia. In another .5 mile you reach the loop junction that you encountered on your way in. Your car is parked .2 mile on your right.

13

Day Pond Loop

Total Distance: 4 miles
Time: 2½ hours
Rating: C
Highlights: A fully developed state park, trout pond
Map: USGS 7½' Moodus

New England's forests, rock formations, and hills make a very nice setting for our hikes. We even have one feature that is world famous and almost unique — our glorious fall colors! Westerners may rave about their yellow aspen — we not only have yellows but a riot of other colors that are beautiful in themselves and glorious together. What a grand and pleasant surprise it must have been for the Pilgrims to be greeted their first New England fall in 1621 by our magnificent colors!

Around Labor Day the sumac and the red maple turn red and scarlet. Then the yellow of popples (related to the West's aspens) and birch appear, followed by seemingly translucent ash (perhaps our favorite) with deep purple on top of the leaf and yellow beneath — the wind sets off this two-toned effect beautifully. Our crown jewels, the sugar maples with their fantastic range of hues from yellow through orange to brilliant reds, burst into brilliance, and finally the various oaks with their deep long-lasting rusts complete the tapestry.

The only area in the world with colors to rival ours is eastern China, but our far greater number of trees makes New En-

gland's show unprecedented. You may wonder why only these two areas, half a world apart, are so blessed. One reasonable theory is that many millions of years ago between ice ages, at a time when our present trees were developing, Greenland was a warm forested island which served as a bridge over the pole between northern Asia and North America. The return of the ice pushed the forest south into both areas — the color genes were thus derived from a single source and spread into both eastern China and eastern North America. Hence our somewhat equivalent color displays.

To get to Day Pond, take exit 16 off Route 2 and go south on CT 149. In three miles turn right at the "Day Pond State Park" sign. After another .4 mile you reach the park entrance on your right. There is ample angle parking along the road around the pond.

Several water-loving swamp maples surround the entrance. Various oaks and the yellow-foliaged tulip trees are found here. Follow the dirt entrance road around the pond on your left past a large rainy-day picnic shelter, also on your left. There are a few outhouses scattered about but the next building (again on your left) is an elaborate rest room facility complete with water fountain. Such development is both bad and good. It means that the state is acquiring very few new parks and can thus put most of its money into developing existing parks. (Note: the multi-year, multi-million dollar Heritage program started in the mid-1980s aspires to double Connecticut's recreational land base before the century is out.)

After curving around the beach and adjacent dressing rooms turn right by a pair of outhouses just before the dam. The blue-blazed trail heads down hill on an old tote road. If you choose the latter part of October for this hike you will find that the shorter hours of daylight (not the frost) have painted the foliage lavishly with a spectrum of reds and orange.

In a few yards the trail turns sharply

glacial erratic

Westchester

0.5   1.0 mile

left off the tote road; you are still following the blue blazes. Jog slightly left and cross the natural gas pipeline easement; continue downhill toward the stream.

The outlet stream from Day Pond lends a cheery background to the first part of this hike. The stream moves quickly downhill matching the trail, thus forming a series of small falls and rapids on its way to the Salmon River. Less than ½ mile from the pond, we turn sharply right uphill away from the stream on the blue-blazed trail (where we turn, the blue trail also goes left, crosses the brook, climbs uphill and joins the road that bisects the Day Pond Loop).

It is interesting to note the young beech at this turn in our path. Depending upon how late in the autumn you are walking, many of the trees may have lost their foliage. The red maple leaves are often off before the other colors are fully developed. The various oaks will usually hold their leaves well into the winter. However, the young (but not the old) beech will often hold their leaves into early spring. By then the leaves are bleached almost white but are still holding on.

Cross under the power lines and climb until you reach a rocky knoll nearly a mile from the start. The rock-strewn area (glacial erratics) culminates in a small, circular, almost flat top. The path starts down the other side where a few cedars still reach the sun.

After several minor ups and downs, the trail leaves its mostly northern direction and heads west downhill crossing a stone wall. Upon reaching a woodland valley you go along the left side following the blue blazes. As the valley cuts deeper into the local water table a stream becomes visible, which grows as

Day Pond

the valley deepens. Soon you cross the stream.

The valley and its stream end at a deeper valley and larger stream coming directly from Day Pond. At the bottom of a hill the rough tote road you have been following hits a well-defined old road where the trail turns left. After crossing the stream again (the smaller stream that you followed down the valley) and starting up a gentle grade, the blue-blazed trail turns right.

Follow the blue trail into the woods, then right again and finally left across the larger stream from Day Pond. You are now better than halfway around the circuit. Go left along the bank of this stream beside a stone wall. Soon go right uphill away from the brook. Cross under the power line and wind slowly upward through what, at first glance, appears to be an almost featureless woodland. However, our woodlands are never featureless! Along here we saw a large expanse of white pine and eastern hemlock, a young deciduous woodland, and acres of club mosses—many carrying their spore stalks like banners.

After almost a mile of gentle upgrade you crest a rocky knoll and then cross a linear clearing carrying a transcontinental cable. After crossing a small, mostly dry-bottomed valley, the blue-blazed trail resumes its gentle upward slope.

Pass at right a 200-ton glacial erratic. Besides a patina of algae and lichen, this great rock supports a young black birch on its top and a clump of polypody fern clinging to a foothold on its side. Estimating such things as the weight of this boulder, the grains of sand on a beach, or the number of leaves on a large tree can be approximated quite handily by taking a small section and multiplying by the whole—you will definitely not be exact, but you will have a good idea of the actual number. For this boulder we estimated its weight as about 200 pounds per cubic foot (water is about 64 pounds per cubic foot) and its size as twenty feet square by ten feet high. A simple calculation produces a weight of 400,000 pounds or 200 tons.

As you reach the end of the loop the path meets, parallels, and then crosses a stone wall. You soon cross an old tote road whose dirt surface is below much of the surrounding land—erosion from past heavy use! Shortly you reach the park road just south of the dam.

You then cross the pond's outlet stream on two bridges, pass the two outhouses (left) where you started the loop hike, and retrace your steps to your car.

The two consecutive bridges over the pond's outlets are particularly interesting and show that the dam's designer knew what he was doing. The smaller stream's outlet in the dam is lower so that it will always carry some of the pond's overflow with its cheery burble. The second outlet is higher but much wider than the first. In case of heavy floods this can hold a large amount of water while the smaller dam is limited. The two outlets prevent an unacceptable water build-up against the dam which could result in overflow and increased erosion if the smaller outlet was unable to drain off the accumulating water. This pond then has the best of both worlds—it has the advantage of a small compact outlet while having a safety valve which comes into play in case of heavy floods.

14

Sunny Valley

Total Distance: 3 miles
Time: 2 hours
Rating: C
Features: Fading glacial pond, hemlock forest, and
*   abandoned mine*
Map: USGS 7½' New Milford, Roxbury

A hike can be far more than just a bit of exercise in the woods or a chance to chin with a variety of like-minded folks. The woods are a wonderland where your depth of understanding can have no limit. The trees, the low-slung plants, the animals of chance encounter, the geologic clues, and signs of man's doings are all there for us to see. The nicest thing about "reading from nature" is that for the ever-curious amateur naturalist, there are no tests, no one to satisfy—except yourself! Some things are seasonal, some are around for decades, some date to colonial times, and still others go back to the ice ages and beyond. An encyclopedia would be needed to detail each hike you take, especially if you look closely and during all seasons. We will touch briefly in this hike on three of these categories of wonder—the ice-ages, trees, and traces left by colonial man.

Sunny Valley Foundation in Bridgewater, founded to revitalize New England agriculture, provides trails as one facet of its multiple-use land management scheme. The Foundation's properties encompass nearly 1,500 acres; trails are maintained on about 480 acres with over 1,000 acres managed as natural areas, woodlands, and farmlands.

From the junction of CT routes 67 and 133 in Bridgewater, go south on CT 133 about .7 mile then turn right on Hat Shop Hill Road. After .6 mile, jog left then right on Hemlock Road for 1.6 miles to the end of the pavement. Continue .2 mile to the small parking lot at left just before the Stony Brook Farm entrance.

Our trail starts at the sign "Silica Mine Hill" in the rear right corner of the parking area. Start up the gentle grade through the cedar gate on the white-blazed trail. Shortly our path levels and proceeds along an old farm road before climbing again. Gradually the grade steepens before reaching a white trail on the right. Take the white trail which goes down gradually through hemlocks then slabs the hillside which drops off steeply to the right.

Hemlock forests tell an interesting story. Look beneath this dense stand of hemlocks. The thick acid bed of fallen needles and twigs and the tightly interwoven, light-intercepting foliage has

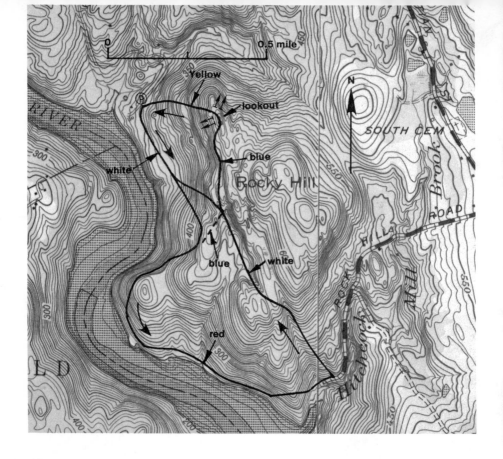

banished all other plants from the forest floor until only young hemlocks can grow. Connecticut's climax forest will then be maintained until fire, axe, or other catastrophe allows another cycle to start.

Soon you come to a blue connecting trail at left; continue on the white trail, but watch carefully as the white trail turns right downhill soon after the blue trail junction. Clearly many people have missed this turn as the trail appears to go straight for about fifty feet beyond the turn, but dies as it approaches a stone wall. The trail is lovely and soft underfoot thanks to the hemlock needles covering the ground.

After moderating, our trail again turns right and heads steeply downhill, reaching a little saddle. Go uphill on the white

trail, resisting the temptation to go right on the easy downhill. After another dip, our well-marked trail turns left and continues on a steady down. Soon Lake Lillinonah is visible through the trees below. Reaching the shore, motor boats may be seen racing through the narrows. Continue in the trees in sight of the lake on your right. As we walked we came on a group of three tents at the water's edge. Evidently some folks brought gear in by boat and were enjoying a glorious weekend "away from it all."

When you begin to ascend away from the lake, go through a deliberate break in an old stone wall and soon hit a dirt road (posted at right)—go left on the road (coming from the other direction, there is a trail sign). Watch carefully, just before you reach another old road, go left slightly uphill on the white-blazed trail. The white trail goes sharply right towards the inlet (if you follow the white to the next junction before looping back you extend the hike another 1.5 miles).

Climb steadily on the old road through an area that has been logged fairly recently. Near the top of the rise our white trail goes right away from the road. The footway is not well-worn and logging remains obscure the path, but it is well-blazed and soon you climb out of this area, passing ledge outcroppings at right. As you climb, notice the deep hollow at right that gradually gets shallower as you reach the height of land.

As you descend, Lost Pond appears on the right. The thought may cross your mind (as it did ours) that it should have stayed lost. It is a mucky, slimy long narrow water hole which is gradually being lost to succession. In winter, it's a lovely spot, but in summer, it's a mosquito breeding ground with little to recommend it.

The glaciers that covered our area

Looking west from The Lookout

over 10,000 years ago left many traces. There are thousands of these geological reminders in Connecticut—glacial erratics, old kettleholes, and dying ponds. The drying, long narrow pond here on the side of the mountain is such a remnant. The gouging glacier helped form this water-holding trench, whose bottom is relatively impervious to water. The natural demise of all ponds sooner or later has pushed this one far towards its evolutionary end. Aquatic vegetative growth, wind- and water-borne debris have all contributed to the filling in of the pond. The scum on its surface and the trail wending through its former outlet are signs of its return to dry land.

Soon our trail swings left away from the pond and goes down along what appears to have been the pond outlet in years past. Drop down and keep a sharp eye out as our trail bears right through fern groves and goes directly across the shallow area to a rock outcrop. Shortly come to an old silica mine at right—see the silicon dioxide-quartz rocks around an old mine hole. This abandoned silica mine is indicative of the lack of mineral wealth in Connecticut. When our state was first settled, dreams of mineral wealth led to much part-time prospecting in Connecticut. Limited amounts of cobalt, iron ore, garnets, silica, and even traces of gold lured these early prospectors. Most of the holes they dug have filled in. In a few places some small successes caused larger diggings where activity faded before the richer lodes elsewhere. This silica mine is a case in point. Like other local mines it's just a relic of the past to stimulate our curiosity.

Pass more quartz and silica rocks all along the trail. Soon after rock outcroppings at left, a blue connector trail comes in at left. Just after that a trail to the right leads to another silica mine hole. Continue on the white trail going between huge rock slabs and an old cellar hole at right. When you reach the blue trail at right, take it uphill toward the lookout. Climb steadily but gradually past large stone slabs to the lookout with good views to the west.

As you leave the lookout, go left downhill on the yellow-blazed trail through mountain laurel. Soon come to an old road which you follow left with the yellow blazes through another hemlock forest. When you reach the dirt road, go left about 100 yards to your car.

15

Northwest Park

Total Distance: 3.8 miles
Time: 2½ hours
Rating: CD
Highlights: Tobacco barns, Interpretive Nature Center with live
  animal exhibits, self-guided nature trail for the blind,
  Tobacco Museum
Map: USGS 7½' Windsor Locks

A major feature of the Connecticut River Valley is fading fast. Our world-famous crop of shade-grown tobacco, once the highest valued agricultural crop in the country, is about gone. In the late thirties, Windsor alone had 3,000 acres of shade-grown tobacco. Over 1,600 square miles of tobacco, under its head-high cover of shade-cloth, were found in the Connecticut River Valley and dominated the landscape long after World War II. Cheaper tobacco from other countries, a reduction in the number of smokers, and the astronomical increase in the value of the land for housing have all contributed to the near extinction of our shade-grown tobacco.

Most of the state's thousands of imposing tobacco barns, where the crop was dried before use as top-quality cigar wrappers, were torn down for their weathered lumber which, ironically, was extensively used in the same houses that contributed to the decline of this valuable crop. One of the special features of this hike is the still looming presence of tobacco barns. A generation ago these barns were everywhere and familiar to any Nutmegger. Now

they are about gone, but here we pass several of these reminders of bygone days on this property now owned by the Town of Windsor.

This park of more than 400 acres includes 8.2 miles of trail, but the hike we chose is about 3.8 miles long. To get to Northwest Park, take exit 38 from I-91 (about 7 miles north of Hartford). Go north on CT Route 75 (Poquonock Ave.) for about 1.4 miles, then turn left onto Prospect Hill Road. After 1.2 miles, go right on Lang Road. Continue .4 mile to the parking lot at the entrance to Northwest Park.

Walk past the small pond to the Interpretive Nature Center (open 12-5 Monday through Thursday, 10-3 Saturday; call for summer hours; no admission charge). You may want to wait until after your hike to visit the center, but do go in before you leave. Go down the dirt road to the left of the Nature Center (playground at left) past the old tobacco barns. Follow the signs straight ahead to the Bog, Hemlock, and Pond Trails—there is a picnic area at right. Shortly the Pond (and Wetland Forest) Trail goes straight, but you go left toward the Bog Trail on an old road.

The Bog Trail is a .6 mile long Braille trail "dedicated to the memory of Merlin W. Sargent in appreciation of his many years of service to American Youth Hostels-Yankee Council." The guide rope will conduct you around the bog and return you to the starting point. Since the day we scouted this trail was warm and humid (ideal mosquito weather), we decided to continue straight ahead to the Hemlock Trail. Our decision was reinforced when a solitary hiker came by saying, "I just tripped over a mosquito in the bog!" However, in cooler weather, this is a delightful trail.

The guide rope and our road run together for about .1 mile and you continue beyond the Braille trail straight ahead to the Hemlock Trail marked with white blazes. Follow the white blazes left and soon you once again briefly join the Braille trail. Go through the gated chain-link fence designed to keep vehicles out. The trail is delightfully soft underfoot thanks to the ground covering of needles—a fleeting phenomena as oak trees already rise above the hemlocks. Switchback downhill noticing the mole tunnels crossing the trail along the way. Stay on the white blazed trail going through another chain-link fence before reaching the Pond Trail junction.

At the junction go straight ahead on the blue-blazed Pond Trail and soon loop right uphill and then down again. Stop and rest a moment at the large sitting log at left, then cross an old log bridge (which may be slippery). Look out at the pond ahead then bear right on another wood bridge before bearing right uphill.

At the top of the hill, you go left on the yellow Wetland Forest Trail. If you go straight, the blue and yellow trails run together until you reach a dirt road which leads to the Nature Center in less than .5 mile. Continue on the yellow trail downhill, soon crossing an old road as the trail levels out. Soon after passing a large boulder at right you catch glimpses of the Farmington River below at left. When you reach the field, you have a choice—either edge the field (and risk poison ivy) or stay in the woods on a trail with a sign that warns "X-C skiers—Danger—Steep Trail." For hikers the trail is no problem, but you'll miss the wild strawberries that dot the field in late June.

When you reach the next junction, leave the Wetland Forest Trail and continue straight on the green Connector Trail "A." At left there are intermittent views of the river as you drop down to the riverbank. Soon the trail goes right and you cross a wooden footbridge before meeting the pink Rainbow Reservoir Trail. Go right back toward the Center (going straight takes you on the Rainbow Reservoir loop and adds nearly 2 miles to the hike). Shortly you come to the orange blazes of the Softwood Forest Trail—go left. Soon the pink and orange trails run together as they go to the right along an old road. Continue slightly uphill past a big beech tree at left and then go right as our orange trail splits away from the Rainbow Reservoir Trail. The needles are soft underfoot, but the hardwoods are beginning to shade out the softwoods here.

The trail twists and turns its way until you come to a small bridge—cross the bridge and at the junction, go left on the yellow Wetland Forest Trail. Here the white birches are dead or dying. Cross a woods road and continue on the yellow blazes. When you come to the Wetland Forest trailhead, go left on an old road .2 mile past the tobacco barn to the Nature Center.

16

Newgate Prison

Total Distance: 4 miles
Time: 2½ hours
Rating: C
Highlights: Historic Newgate Prison, views
Map: USGS 7½' Windsor Locks

Choose a cool, clear day for this hike. It begins with a pleasant walk along the traprock ridge of the northern Metacomet Trail, then descends into the valley to explore the forbidding environs of infamous Newgate Prison, and finally returns to the start along a well-shaded country road.

To reach the hike's start, follow CT 20 west .7 mile from its junction with CT 187 in Granby to Newgate Road on the right. Go north on Newgate Road a little way until you see the blue-blazed Metacomet Trail enter the woods at right. There is room to park on the road. The path climbs steeply onto the traprock ridge and then bears left along the top.

In leafless season the views here are particularly nice, but even in summer you catch glimpses of the countryside below through occasional breaks in the trees. The utility line you soon pass beneath services a string of ridgetop beacons for planes approaching Bradley International Airport just to the east. The airplane buff will appreciate the procession of 727s, 737s, 747s, DC-10s, DC-8s, and a myriad of smaller private aircraft that come and go overhead.

In a little under one mile the trail emerges onto a lookout about 300 feet above the valley floor. The USGS benchmark reads Copper Mountain. The Tunxis Trail follows the traprock ridge across the road directly opposite you; to the left stretches the sinuous ridge curve the Metacomet Trail follows. Heublein Tower (see Hike 37) stands out prominently; Penwood State Park (see Hike 21) straddles the nearest hump; and past the tower the tilted slabs of Mount Higby (see Hike 29) rise on the horizon.

Still on the ridge, the trail descends slowly and steadily and then climbs again. Nearly two miles from the start you reach an excellent lookout ledge with fine views to the west. Below you and to the south, there is a small paved road circle. Continue on the trail, soon coming to a grassy spot which overlooks the scree slope.

Retrace your steps to your car, and then follow Newgate Road for a little over a mile.

Before long you come to the impressive ruins of Newgate Prison on your right. Originally the site of the first copper smelter in America (circa 1705), the mine was pressed into service as a prison just before the Revolutionary War.

View from the Metacomet Trail

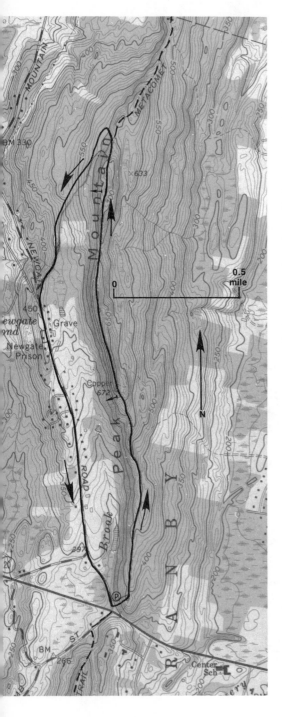

It became most famous as a prison for Tories during the war. The prison is open daily from Memorial Day through October. There is a small entrance fee.

For a short excursion into the seamier side of our nation's past, join the line of waiting visitors. After descending 50 feet in a narrow shaft, you enter the mine proper. Water seeps down the walls. A motley crew of Tories, thieves, and debtors were forced to live and labor in this cavernous prison while fettered with leg irons, handcuffs, and iron collars. Marks worn on the floor by pacing prisoners are still visible two centuries later, and tales of barbarity seem to echo in the hollow chambers.

After exploring the prison, return to Newgate Road. The fresh air will be especially welcome after the dusty dungeon. Keeping right (south), continue down the shaded, open road to your car.

17

Chatfield Hollow

Total Distance: 5.5 miles
Time: 3 hours
Rating: C
Highlights: Views, state park featuring fresh water swimming
Maps: USGS 7½' Clinton, Haddam

Hikers may complain about the overuse of a few select areas, yet Connecticut's trails are for the most part underused. As throughout the east, the Appalachian Trail is heavily traveled while most other trails are often practically deserted. If you feel that one of the joys of hiking is temporarily leaving behind the clamor of fellow human beings, consider Chatfield Hollow State Park. Despite several hundred carloads of people in the park on a summer weekend, on our visits we met only two youngsters and a group from the New Haven Hiking Club on this park's well-maintained trails.

Chatfield Hollow lies within that wide band of woodland separating the overdeveloped shore from the inland tier of cities. From the junction of CT 80 and CT 81 in Killingworth, drive west one mile on CT 80. The park entrance is on your right.

Follow the tar road around Schreeder Pond to the parking area on the far side of Oak Lodge Shelter on the west side of the pond near the dam. The pond, which offers fishing, swimming, and picnicking, is the focus of park activity. Walk away from the tar road south, away from the pond, for a short distance and turn right into the woods (opposite a small grove of white pine trees) on the orange-blazed Deep Woods Trail.

The trail moves up a rocky slope atop which there are open rock ledges decorated with mountain laurel. Whenever we mention mountain laurel to people they often exclaim that they will have to go there in June to catch the display of gorgeous flowers. However, any one twig of mountain laurel blooms at best every other year, so you could conceivably have half the flowers in bloom each year. Most areas have a great year followed by a so-so year when most twigs are busily putting their energy into new growth instead of flowers. Once an area's pattern is known to you, you can usually depend upon hitting the great flowering every other year; mid to late June is the best time.

In .5 mile from the start, the trail curves left off the ledges, then passes beneath them. The ledge's rock faces are stained with mosses and lichens and trees sprout from great cracks. You can use lichens as an indicator of air quality; an abundance of lichens signifies clean air, whereas pollution inhibits their growth and can even kill them.

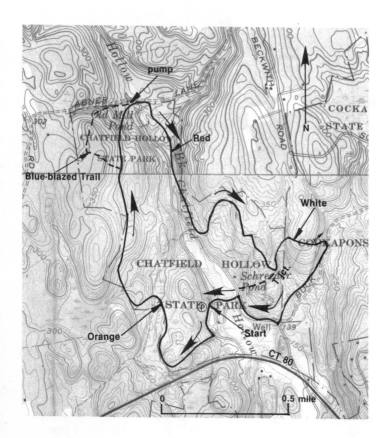

Near a small brook crossing, a park naturalist has attached signs to many trees—among them white cedar, yellow birch, black birch, witch hazel, chestnut, white oak, red oak, sassafras, blue beech, American beech, pignut hickory, white ash, flowering dogwood, and tupelo or black gum. Most of the signs are in this area, but we saw a few odd signs scattered throughout the park.

Not very far from here Gerry caught and released a hognose snake. This snake is so safe to handle that it makes the common garter snake look dangerous. When accosted, this slow-moving species will stop, flatten its head and throat, hiss, and otherwise threaten you.

If this ploy doesn't work, then it will writhe, turn over "dead" and loll its tongue. From all appearances it is dead, but if you turn it onto its stomach, it will promptly roll over onto its back—a "dead" snake must be belly up! It will only play dead for a while before it will again try to flee. The most annoying thing about these snakes, which we've never known to bite, is the foul-smelling fluid they leave on your skin when handled—it can take some time before this smell is worn or washed away.

After passing a blue-blazed trail twice, the 1.5 mile orange-blazed trail ends at a tar park road well beyond Schreeder Pond. Enjoy a refreshing drink from a

Waterwheel at Chatfield Hollow

hand-pump (left) then proceed left along the road, across the bridge, and around the east side of the dammed pool to pick up the red-blazed Ridge Trail. Initially this footpath parallels the stream, passes a breast water-wheel (an undershot wheel where the water strikes the middle of the wheel, then its falling weight turns the wheel) and a covered bridge. Then the trail curves left uphill through pines.

The red-blazed trail continues generally uphill, passing beside and on top of several ledges. Finally it turns left steadily uphill. After a few yards the trail curves back on itself. The trail system inside this park does a marvelous job of twisting and winding through and along the most interesting areas. The trail levels a bit, climbs steeply again and emerges on top of a ledge after passing around the left end of this large almost perpendicular rock wall.

At a "T" follow the red blazes left. The trail passes alongside a wet rock wall. In another .25 mile you pass beside (left) a layered rock wall and then climb fairly steeply up a rocky slope. The red-blazed trail soon curves back, passing alongside another layered rock wall (right). Finally the trail reaches the top of this gneiss ledge and goes back sharply along the top. In a little way you'll find yourself on the white blazed Look Out Trail. Bear left (north) on the white trail to include this trail in your hike. If you go right, you'll soon hit Buck Road and then the paved entrance road having completed about 4.5 miles.

In another .25 mile the white trail hits an open ledge with a cameo view down the valley. Eventually you come out onto a ledge with a nice view south that encompasses Foster Ponds south of CT 80. The trail then curves around to the right and zigzags steeply down the slope. It pauses now and again and levels off to take you to a particularly appealing area. Passing through some small mostly dead hemlocks you soon reach a junction—go left downhill.

Several times on your left you will glimpse a gravel road (Buck Road) as you tend downhill. This continues until you spot the junction of Buck Road with the park's tar entrance road that you came in on. Go though some pines to the tar road, then go right. Follow the tar road—at its junction with another tar road, go left. At the sharp southeast corner of Schreeder Pond, go left along the pond's dam to your car.

18

Soapstone

Total Distance: 4.2 miles
Time: 2½ hours
Rating: C
Highlights: Upland woods, views
Map: USGS 7½' Ellington

Soapstone—an intriguing name for a mountain—sits in the midst of the 6,000-acre Shenipsit State Forest. A quarry on the east slope used by Indians and early settlers once yielded the soft, talc-like, greasy, lustered stone from which the mountain derives its name. In colonial times, this stone was valued for its high heat retention; flannel-wrapped hot soapstones lessened the shock of icy bedclothes.

Soapstone Mountain is located east of the Connecticut River in Somers. From the junction of CT 140 and CT 83 drive north on CT 83 for 4 miles to Parker Road and turn right. After 1.3 miles (the last .4 mile is a rough three-season dirt road) turn right again onto dirt Soapstone Mountain Road. There is limited parking on the left in .4 mile where the blue-blazed Shenipsit Trail crosses the road.

Follow the trail east (to the right). (The blue-blazed route west leads to the beginning of the northern section of the Shenipsit Trail about 3 miles south.) The forest you hike through has a lovely, soothing sameness. An understory of maple and black birch struggle for sunlight in the gaps between large red oaks. The leaf-littered floor is carpeted with masses of ground pine and wild lily-of-the-valley. Many of Connecticut's forest are, like this one, all of a size. The last great cutovers were in the early years of this century, and since then cutting has been sporadic—far less than the annual growth—resulting in many trees across the state being about the same age.

Not long after leaving Soapstone Road, you reach the first of many trail junctions. At this one bear right. Watch your turns as there are many paths and old tote roads in this forest. If you are wool-gathering or taking the path of least resistance, it is very easy to miss a turn or two and find that the worn path that you are traveling is devoid of blue blazes. In that event, retrace your steps to the last blaze and try again.

In late spring there are at least two aspects of the vegetation that you may have noticed and wondered about. One is the many groups of star flowers. Spreading mostly by means of underground rhizomes, they are usually found in large stands or not at all. There seem to be more multi-blossom plants here than usual. Secondly, you may think the compact masses of moss have grown hair. Actually, in late spring, moss sends up flowering stalks which allow the resulting spores to spread further after they ripen.

The fairly smooth path steepens, becomes rockier, climbs a small rocky defile, and curves right. About .2 mile from the start, you have a partial view south when the leaves are off the trees. However, this and similar views grow dimmer and more obscure with continued forest growth.

We passed through here once at a magic time of year—the small leaflets bursting from their winter buds had spread a delicate, light green blush over the forested hills. A week earlier and the hills would still have a stark wintry look; a week later and inexorable growth would have clothed all. This is the easiest phenomenon to miss—the brief, precious moment of transition.

At .7 mile you cross Parker Road and shortly bear left. The swamp at left is happy in spring, echoing with the high pitched chorus of spring peepers. We have all heard countless thousands of these diminutive tree frogs with the big voice, but have you ever seen one in song? Cautious creeping in the evening with the subtle use of a flashlight may reward you with the sight of one of these small tan frogs, whose throat swells into a great white bubble-like soundbox from a body less than an inch long. Summer sightings are more a matter of quick eyes, quicker hands, and luck. Most of the woodland hoppers you find are the black-masked wood frogs, but occasionally you will find a tiny frog without the mask and a faint contrasting "X" on his back—this is the spring peeper.

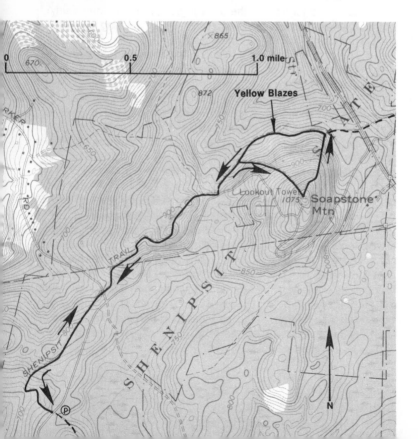

Observation tower on Soapstone Mountain

The trail ascends another rocky outcropping over upward-tipped ledges. This is gneiss, the basic bedrock of much of Connecticut which was laid down in flat layers hundreds of millions of years ago. These protruding ledges were tilted by subsequent crystal deformations.

In spring, fern fiddleheads pop up everywhere. Instead of growing gradually like most annuals, the fern uncoils like a New Year's Eve favor from a tightly curled mass into a fully grown plant. In northern New England the fiddleheads of the ostrich fern are considered a delicacy. We are told that our common cinnamon fern fiddlehead is also good to eat but you have to remove all the light brown fuzz before you can eat it—seeing what a job that is, we have never tried it, nor have we found anyone who has!

The trail has been rolling gradually upward and after 1.1 miles reaches the summit of rocky West Soapstone Mountain (930 feet). Near the top in spring you may find an atypical species of violet, the northern downy violet. The leaves are long, oval, and fuzzy rather than the more familiar heart-shaped and smooth, but the familiar violet-blue flowers are unmistakable. There are dozens of species of violets, and with hybridization even the experts have trouble with some identifications. So we have a ready-made excuse if we cannot identify a violet—it must be a hybrid!

On a leafless day, the microwave tower on the main summit of the main peak of Soapstone Mountain appears across the valley. The trail works downhill and near the bottom is steep and badly eroded by trail bikes. You pass quite near Sykes Road on the right before joining a tote road that leads you downhill. The blue trail leaves the road .5 mile from the west summit and heads to the right up the main peak of Soapstone Mountain—a good steady climb. (The yellow blazes on the continuation of the tote road bypass the summit and rejoin the blue trail in about .4 mile.) Climbing, you reach the top (1,075 feet) 1.9 miles from your start.

This summit is a good example of the sometimes rapid effects rendered by the hand of man. When we first wrote about this summit in 1977, the old fire tower that we had used so many times had been removed as unsafe, but the following year an observation tower was erected in its place. Now (1990) vandals' graffiti is all over this structure, but it still offers wonderful views.

An easy climb of the observation tower presents a bird's-eye view of the surrounding country. Off to the west is the flat valley land. To the north and south is the well-wooded mountain ridge of which Soapstone is a prominent part.

The trail down from the summit is a bit obscure due to removal of trees, a handy marking media. You enter the woods just to the left of the telephone line. Your route threads through an attractive field of glacial erratics. After .3 mile, turn left on the yellow-blazed tote road (the blue-blazed Shenipsit Trail continues to the Massachusetts border about six miles farther on).

The yellow trail route describes a shallow bowl with a bent lip. Go up the lip, dip gently into the bowl with its rather wet bottom, and rise gently to the junction with the blue trail that you came in on. Proceed straight ahead on the blue trail, retracing your steps 1.6 miles to your car.

19

9/19/98

Beautiful sunny day —
Some fish breaking on beach —
Guilford Fair —

Bluff Point

Total Distance: 4.5 miles
Time: 2¼ hours
Rating: D
Highlights: Undeveloped beach, ocean views
Map: USGS 7½' New London

A combination of historical circumstances and heavy demand for shoreline property has kept most of Connecticut's short coastline inaccessible to the general public. Of the very few state parks on this shore, the 778-acre, undeveloped Bluff Point State Park is a special place for the walker. The only such sizeable acreage on the Connecticut coast, Bluff Point is free from concessions, cottages, picnic tables, and campsites.

There are no signs to direct you to Bluff Point. From the intersection of CT 117 and US 1 in Groton, drive west for .3 mile on US 1 to Depot Road. Turn left, following this street past Industrial Road and under the railroad tracks (where the paved surface ends) until you reach a closed gate about .7 mile from US 1. You know that you have arrived when you spy a sign listing park regulations. There is an area designated for parking on the right side of the gate.

Proceed on foot down the gated dirt road. Fishing boats ply the bay to your right, and windrows of dead eelgrass, one of the few flowering plants that grow in salt water, line the rocky shore. The brant, a smaller relative of the Can-

ada goose, feeds almost exclusively on this plant. When a mysterious blight in the 1930s all but exterminated the eelgrass, the brant nearly went too. The emaciated flocks subsisted on a diet of sea lettuce until the grass came back. If you walk this way in the colder months, you may see a few of the hundreds of brant that winter along the shore of Long Island Sound.

Numerous side paths cut off from the main road. Due to the all-pervading influence of the sea, the woods of Bluff Point are more varied than most inland forests. The tangle of vines and brambles — grape, red-fruited barberry, rose, blackberry, black raspberry, honeysuckle, Oriental bittersweet, and greenbriar — is thick enough to make any Br'er Rabbit feel at home. Various oaks, cherries, long-thorned hawthorns, tight-barked hickories, shag-bark hickories, sumacs, and blueberries represent the deciduous trees, and an occasional cedar represents the evergreen trees.

You will probably see one or more swans gracing the bay on this hike. They will almost certainly be European mute swans. These birds descended from escaped captives from various es-

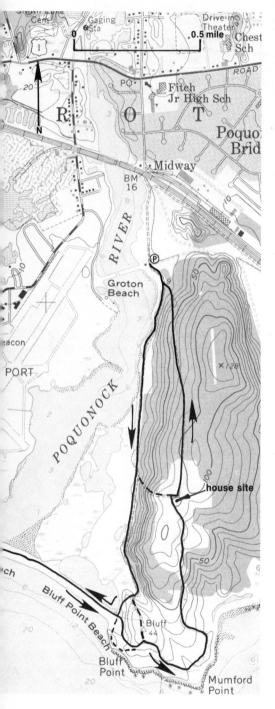

tates (mostly on Long Island). These descendants are now spreading rapidly throughout the waterways of the northeast.

During an April visit you may hear the mating chorus of the male peepers and toads. These dry-land dwellers congregate, upon breaking hibernation, in various temporary waters to breed. The peeper has a high-pitched two-note call, hence its name. The toad produces a long trill. If these amphibians mistakenly choose a permanent body of water in which to lay their eggs, various water-dwelling enemies will devour the tadpoles; if the pools they select dry up too soon, the tadpoles will die before complete metamorphosis. As with many things in nature, a very delicate balance exists.

The most common tree in this narrow strip of woodland is probably sassafras, usually recognized by its mitten-shaped leaves and greenish-barked twigs. Sassafras leaves usually come in three shapes—like a mitten with no thumb, one thumb, or two thumbs—often on the same branch. As a rule, those leaves nearest the end of a twig have the least "thumbs." Bark peeled from sassafras roots is used to make a strong tea which, according to folklore, purifies the body. Unfortunately, every Eden has its snake—recent studies have shown that one of the common ingredients of this tea causes cancer in laboratory animals.

About 1.5 miles from your start, you reach the low bluffs on a point of land. Over the water to your right lies Groton Heights, and to your left, Groton Long Point. Fisher's Island, part of New York State, lies to the right of center, while Watch Hill in Rhode Island is at left of center.

A bit before the bluff a boardwalk on your right detours you onto Bluff Point beach. Wander down this beach a bit

Beach flora

before continuing your exploration of Bluff Point itself. Castoff treasures from the sea await your curious gaze: rope, great blocks of wood, blue mussel shells, great whorled whelk shells, marble-sized periwinkle shells, scallop shells, shells from long razor clams, flat wide strands of kelp, bladder floated algae (seaweed), crab husks, and the everlasting, ever-present plastics—the bane of all the world's oceans.

When you have satisfied your yen for beach walking or have reached the end of this beach, retrace your steps, following sprawling masses of delicate beach peas back to the bluff. Before you start around this point, pause for a moment among the wild primroses and beach plums. You are standing on a terminal moraine. This hasty-pudding mix of rocks and sand was dumped here some ten thousand years ago when the glacier that completely covered present-day New England retreated.

Follow the road around to the east. Soon after leaving the shore, take the better-worn path (inland) left; at the fork 50 yards further on, bear right (the trail to the left soon connects with the outward-bound leg of your hike). Rounding the point, you look over a cattail swamp which is being taken over throughout the state by the giant reed phragmites (pronounced frag-mi-tez), their waving plumes standing sentinel by the sound. Across the bay, a seemingly solid wall of cottages stand in stark contrast to this wild oasis.

The trail moves inland to follow the center ridge of the peninsula. Stone walls stand in mute evidence of colonial cultivation. The trail forks after about .5 mile. Near this is the site of the Winthrop house. Built around 1700 by Governor Fitz-John Winthrop, grandson of the famous Massachusetts Bay governor, it had a three-hundred-foot tunnel to the barn and a room-sized brick chimney in the basement for protection from Indian raids.

Leaving this area, take the right fork (the left joins the bayside road you followed earlier). The path tends left until it joins the outbound trail near the parking lot. Go right to your car.

White Memorial Foundation

Total Distance: 4.5 miles
Time: 2½ hours
Rating: D
Highlights: Nature Center, swamp boardwalk
Map: USGS 7½' Litchfield

The 4,000-acre White Memorial Foundation wildlife sanctuary in Litchfield was established in the true spirit of multiple use. Within its boundaries lie over thirty miles of crisscrossing trails, two family campgrounds, a marina, a retail lumber outlet, and the Litchfield Nature Center and Museum. To balance the more unusual sanctuary uses, 200 acres have been set aside in four untouched natural preserves. These areas provide bases against which environmental changes on adjacent tracts can be judged. The easy hike described here explores only a small part of this special sanctuary.

Follow US 202 west 2.2 miles past its junction with CT 118 in Litchfield and turn left by the signs for White Memorial Foundation. The gravel entrance road leads .5 mile to a parking area near the large house that is home to the nature museum (open from 9 AM to 5 PM, Tuesday through Saturday and from 11 AM to 5 PM, Sunday; admission charged).

A rewarding half-hour can be spent looking over the museum's attractive wildlife, geology, and Indian artifact exhibits. A bookstore specializing in natural history sells pamphlets and maps relevant to the area. Since the numerous trails through the foundation's land twist, turn, and cross each other with wild abandon, a map is a good investment.

The maze of dirt roads, trails (marked and unmarked), and byways cross and intercross so much that when you visit this foundation for the first time, you may find following a route difficult. We have even seen expert hikers have trouble following a particular route. However, if you visit this area several times and familiarize yourself with its lovely intricacies, it becomes relatively easy and very rewarding to follow the route we have outlined here.

After parking, continue past the museum down the paved road which soon becomes dirt. Large sugar maples and white ash grace the road to your left. Go straight on a gravel road through a gated entrance blocked by a boulder and flanked by two large cement and stone posts. Keep your eyes peeled for blue blazes as you are now on the Mattatuck Trail, one of Connecticut's blue trails; 6.2 miles of this nearly 35-mile-long trail are within White Memorial Foundation. Soon the road crosses the slow moving Bantam River on a sub-

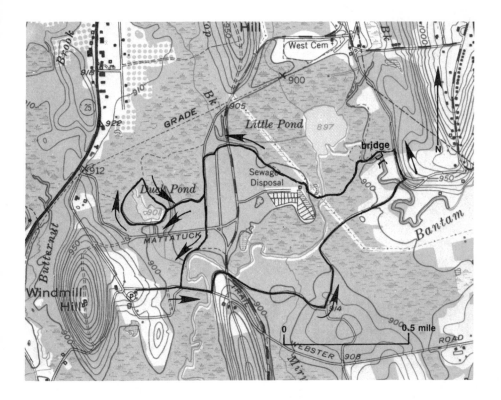

stantial bridge. You may see a passing canoeist or two here. At the end of the bridge, go left following the blue blazes along the woods road. Through the trees, you can see the Bantam River on the left. Hawking dragonflies skim over the water picking up and eating small flying insects such as mosquitos — never hurt a dragonfly!

At your right there is a meadow where a few horses are often seen grazing happily. You may see late summer flowers like Joe-pye weed, boneset, various asters, hawkweed, and purple loosestrife, and hear the strident songs of grasshoppers and crickets near their maximum. The volume from these singers will build up until the first frost: a light frost will slow them, a heavy frost will stop them. The round-leaved cornel,

a species of dogwood with light blue berries, is common here.

Shortly, cross paved Whites Woods Road and enter Catlin Woods on the barred Catlin Road. Pass by a heavy growth of bracken (a fern that must have dry conditions to flourish) and great bull pines (white pines that gained their early growth in the open with little or no competition for the sunlight; the numerous great live branches create the wood known as knotty pine). The trail crosses a dammed-up brook with a desolate appearing pond at right. Soon the woods get dark as sunlight cannot reach the forest floor. The moistness of this area is emphasized by a thick growth of hemlocks. After a bit, white pines mix in more and more until they dominate.

At the junction go left, leaving the blue-blazed trail. The lofty forest around you attests to the superb resiliency of the New England woods. Subject to two major and innumerable minor denudations since 1800, these forests persistently come back. Connecticut has the third highest percentage of forested land in the nation (surpassed only by Maine and New Hampshire).

Our trail, here unmarked, goes gently downhill past some hobblebushes (a viburnum). In spring these large-leaved bushes are graced with flat-topped flower clusters. Look closely; the large showy outer flowers are sterile, the small inner ones produce red, turning to purple, drupes. Hobblebush is more common further north, yet the blooms seem to be more profuse in Connecticut. The fruited bushes already have full-grown long brown buds designed to withstand the winter and usher in the spring with a new crop of leaves.

The trail soon follows a low causeway (an old town road) straight through a partially wooded swamp. It may be quite wet underfoot here. Most of the heavy vegetation encroaching upon the trail consists of various annuals. As the causeway opens you may notice the ever present battle between the native cattails and the alien loosestrife. In 1990, while walking along the causeway, we spotted some Canada geese on the trail just ahead. As we approached, they silently slipped into the swamp waters and disappeared! We knew they were there, but the brown of their necks blended into the brown of the marsh plants in a nearly perfect example of nature's camouflage!

The town road (trail) ends at a golf course which is partly within White Memorial Foundation, so hiking is legal—but watch for flying golf balls! Keep to the left of the mowed area and soon take the path left beside the river (on your right). Continue left, skirting the edge below another hole, and soon cross the river on an arched bridge. Climb part way up the hill on a paved walk and at the end of the pavement, go left on an old grassy woods road. Almost immediately go left into the woods on a slightly overgrown unmarked path. Had you continued on the woods road, you would reach South Lake Street in less than half a mile. Continue on the narrow but well-trodden path, and shortly you're following a stream on your left. At the "T" junction, go left on the Little Pond Trail (LPT) blazed with a black square on a white square. Soon cross the stream on a sturdy bridge and continue right on the LPT. Next you come to a boardwalk which leads to the Frances Howe Sutton bridge.

A boardwalk gives you a fascinating look at one of nature's more interesting but least accessible areas—too wet to walk, too dry to canoe! Jumping frogs, innumerable button bushes, purple loosestrife, royal fern, meadowsweet, lily pads, pickerel weed—in terms of annual increase in vegetation per acre, a swamp is one of the most productive areas.

After leaving the bridge, stay on the black on white blazed boardwalk through the phragmites. At the junction go straight and then immediately left on the Pine Island trail blazed with red triangles. Stay on this trail, soon following the stream again, and shortly cross Whites Woods Road (paved). Continue following the red triangles, turning right at the next junction. These thick, mostly pine and hemlock woods have depos-

Stepping stones across the swamp

ited a soft sound-deadening carpet for you to walk on.

At the next junction go left, and soon, where the red triangles go right, go straight on the blue-blazed Mattatuck Trail. At the fork, stay right on the blue-blazed trail crossing a stream with Duck Pond on the right. Follow the blue blazes where the red triangles go left to Bissell Road. When the Mattatuck Trail goes left, stay straight and soon come to an unmarked trail at right. Take it along the marshy pond, crossing another stream (bridge), then go right once again on the red triangle trail. Watch for the beaver cut trees along the water's edge.

Continue on the boardwalk to the blue Mattatuck Trail and go left following the blue blazes (be careful to turn right at the next intersection). Cross paved Bissell Road and soon go along the Bantam River on your left, soon joining the nature trail which comes in from the right. When the blue trail goes left (you've now completed your circuit), take a right turn back to the museum and your car.

21

Penwood

Total Distance: 4.6 miles
Time: 2½ hours
Rating: C
Highlights: Good views, ridge-top pond
Map: USGS 7½' Avon

The volcanic ridges flanking the Connecticut River Valley offer secluded hiking on the outskirts of the central cities. Penwood State Park sits atop one such ridge. Only a few minutes' drive from Hartford, the trails of Penwood carry you beyond the sights and sounds of our workaday world to a place where the most blatant intrusions are the blue blazes marking your route on the Metacomet Trail.

The park entrance is on the north side of CT 185, one mile west of the CT 185 and CT 178 junction in Bloomfield. There is enough space for a few cars to park on the left just inside the entrance. After the hike, you may want to drive slowly around the tarred circular loop through the park if the road is open.

Pick up the blue blazes of the Metacomet Trail and follow them a short distance down the right hand road (east). Just past a blocked tote road, bear left into the woods, climbing quickly onto the hemlock-shrouded traprock ridge. Once on the top, the trail undulates gently within the forest, which dampens the sounds and sights of our harried world. Even the park road is invisible. Here the thick woods limit the under-growth to a few striped maples, wild sarsaparilla, and maple leaf viburnum.

In 1.8 miles, the trail crosses the tar end of the loop road. Take a break from the hike to explore the little ridge-top pond. Head left across the pavement onto a short boardwalk leading through the swamp and onto the edge of the pond, grandiosely named Lake Louise. The teeming fecundity of life here makes the dry, forested ridge look like a desert.

Discounting the usual forest birds that are drawn to this cornucopia, we saw or heard more varieties of living things in just a few minutes of standing by the pond than in our total time spent on the ridge—dragonflies with outstretched wings, damselflies with folded wings, waterstriders miraculously skimming atop the pond's surface, circling whirligig beetles setting a dizzying circular pace when disturbed, and water boatmen riding just under the water's surface. Gaily colored butterflies displayed marked contrast to the mud perches on which they sat, absorbing moisture from their surroundings. Tadpoles were flitting into sight along the pond's edges when they came up for an occasional gulp of

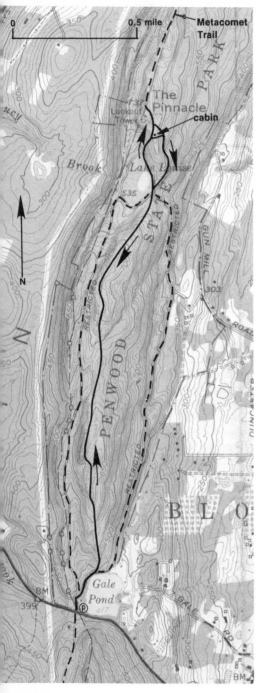

air. Through the water flicked aquatic newts, the adult form of the red efts found on the spring forest floor after a night of gentle rain. Here and there small frogs sat propped up half in and half out of the water, still exhibiting the rounded softness of their recent tadpole stage, and we saw two small water-snakes sunbathing near the boardwalk.

Even the vegetation here is varied and lush. Lily pads dot the surface. Marsh fern, swamp loosestrife, and but-tonbush edge the pond, and a sour gum tree grows on your right. The white blossoms of swamp azaleas perfume the air. Look for the few clumps of swamp Juneberry amid the numerous smooth alders. Their lustrous black berries, which resemble huge huckleberries, make a nice snack. If such a place fas-cinates you as it does us, read the book *Watchers at the Pond* by Francis Russell.

When ready, return to the loop road and continue following the blue blazes left past a huge butternut tree. Follow the blue blazes past an old spring house to the sign that says "Trail" (also double blue blazes). Turn right uphill. Here the steep slope is eased and pro-tected by a long flight of traprock steps. You emerge at the top by a magnificent sealed-off log cabin.

Continue following the blue blazes left to a fine scenic lookout called the Pinna-cle. The ridge traversed by the blue-blazed Tunxis Trail lies to your west across the valley. On the left rises the Heublein Tower (see Hike 37) and fur-ther left the great tilted volcanic slabs of Mount Higby (see Hike 29).

After you have enjoyed the view and perhaps had lunch here, retrace your steps past the front of the sealed-off cabin where you will pick up a tar road.

Follow this road as it zigzags back to the loop road. Here you may go either left or right on the road—either will take you back to your car. Or you may even retrace your steps back over the ridge's central spine to your car.

Lady-slippers

22

Mount Misery

Total Distance: 5.25 miles
Time: 2¾ hours
Rating: CD
Highlights: Views, rhododendron sanctuary, cedar swamp
Maps: USGS 7½' Voluntown, Jewett City

The delightful little summit of Mount Misery belies its name. Set amidst the flat pinelands of Connecticut's largest state forest, this prominent rocky mass adds a nice short climb to an otherwise level hike. Your route to the top, where there are nice views across wooded terrain, follows the Nehantic Trail. This hike picks up the Nehantic Trail on CT 49 in Voluntown. From the intersection of CT 49, CT 165, and CT 138, head east on CT 165 to CT 49 north and turn left. The blue blazes of the trail run along the road. Continue .6 mile to the Beachdale Pond boat launching area parking lot on the right. There is a ramped wharf supplying fishing access for the handicapped. The blue-blazed Nehantic Trail goes off the road into the woods at the double blazes about 100 yards beyond the parking lot.

As you enter the woods, even rows of white and red pine stretch away on either side. These conifers begin to thin out and are replaced by short, scrubby, head-high bushes of bear oak. These trees flourish (if that word may be used for these scraggly specimens) in dry barren soil. Less tolerant but more vigorous trees prevent them from gaining a foothold on richer, deeper soil.

Almost immediately you reach a relatively new paved road; follow it straight ahead. Pass the right turn to the "Office" and soon see scattered blue blazes at left. Very shortly the trail bears right on an old forest road softened by a carpet of pine needles. Next you walk under and then along utility lines before bearing right off this forest road into the woods. The blue-blazed trail here is well-worn and not difficult to follow.

About ½ mile from the start, the Pachaug Trail enters from the right, and the two trails continue as one over Mount Misery. From the trail's junction, proceed downhill bearing left, go under the utility line and continue through the open field to the stone-gated campground road. Cross the road and go through the woods, shortly crossing Mount Misery Brook on a paved road which turns to dirt. Follow the blue-blazed road to the Rhododendron Sanctuary, first passing a playing field which has a pump and excellent drinking water. The trail soon breaks to the right off the road and passes through a grove of young white oaks.

Presently you drop down into a cedar

and rhododendron swamp; you will appreciate the dry, raised trail bed here. Along this stretch of the swamp, jungle-like rhododendron flank the trail. This native evergreen can grow surprisingly tall—to forty feet—and its leathery leaves can reach eight inches in length. The combined effect of all that green is most impressive. In July these huge bushes are dotted with white or pink bell-shaped flowers, creating a spectacular display. Here and there the straight, even boles of tall white cedar thrust through the mass. Their bark is soft and flaky; the greenish tint you see is algae growing on the tree's damp surfaces.

Stay on the blue-blazed trail as other trails loop off it. Soon after the raised trail makes a sharp left and then another, our blue trail goes left into the swamp. Walk lightly, the ground is exceedingly wet and spongy. Follow the blazes carefully and in no time you emerge on a tote road (probably with wet feet). Note carefully where you reached the road, as you will return this way and this turn into the swamp is somewhat obscure. Turn left on the road and in less than ¼ mile, just before a gate and a small pond on the left, the trail bears right off the tote road.

Before you turn, stop and listen. On one mid-March hike here the warm sun beating down on the pond had aroused

Scrub pine on Mount Misery

the resident wood frogs despite the residue from a recent snowfall. Their full, guttural chorus was broken only by the plaintive "peep" of a solitary spring peeper too groggy to give the second half of his familiar call.

Soon you reach a dirt forest road which you follow right for about 50 feet before turning left into the woods again. The level trail passes through oaks and hemlocks. A white cedar with a split down the center large enough to see through stands right in the middle of the trail. What caused this hole? Did two trees once grow together? One of the pleasures of hiking is trying to figure out the reason for such strange phenomena.

The path climbs now, gently at first, to the top of a ridge. Turn left and soon emerge on open rock. Here go right. A singularly misshapen, wind-twisted scrub pine grows on the ledge lookout. This distinctive old friend is one of our favorite trees in Connecticut. Below you can see the open fields where snowmobiles congregate in the winter.

The trail soon drops a bit and crosses a small brook before making its final assault on Mount Misery. The bolts you see in the ledges at the top used to support an abandoned fire tower. The picturesque fire towers dotting the woods of old have been replaced by the more efficient but far less romantic small planes. Although Mount Misery at 441 feet is not very high, the summit provides a fine view of Voluntown, which lies to the far right, while Beachdale Pond is dead center.

On a calm day the open summit ledges also make a fine picnic spot. Be sure to carry out your garbage with you as you retrace your steps to your car.

On your return, as the day grows warm and your legs grow weary, you may shorten your hike and avoid the swamp by going right when you reach the first forest road. Continue on the road and you soon pass a dirt road and then the entrance to the Rhododendron Sanctuary at left and the playing field and pump at right. Here you pick up the blue blazes again and retrace your steps. At the junction of the Nehantic and Pachaug Trails be careful to follow the Nehantic Trail back to your car.

23

Gay City

Total Distance: 5 miles
Time: 2¾ hours
Rating: CD
Highlights: Abandoned town, state park
Map: USGS 7½' Marlborough

Gay City was founded in 1796 by a religious group led by Elijah Andrus. Andrus left town for reasons unknown and in 1800 John Gay, for whom the park was named, was appointed president of the remaining twenty-five families. Even for those times they were an unsociable group; an itinerant peddlar was robbed, murdered and thrown into a town charcoal pit, and a blacksmith's assistant was slain by his employer for failing to show up for work.

The two most prominent families were the Gays and the Sumners, whose rivalry outlasted the town. The Gays called the settlement Gay City, and the Sumners called it Sumner, although it seems the settlement was known locally as Factory Hollow. To further confuse the issue, when the Foster sisters, descendants of the Sumners, deeded the 2,000-acre area to the state in the 1940s, they stipulated that it be called Gay City!

The town's decline, well underway before the Civil War, followed the usual pattern of hardscrabble areas; the old died and the young left. A paper mill outlasted all the houses; when it burned in 1879 the town was gone. Join us in a hike along the now empty dirt roads of this New England ghost town.

Gay City State Park is located off CT 85 just south of the Bolton-Hebron town line. In addition to the ten numbered hiking trails the park offers swimming and picnicking; facilities including outhouses, bathhouses, picnic tables, outdoor fireplaces, and in the summer, an open refreshment stand. There is a fee for parking inside the gates on summer weekends.

Emulating the thrifty Yankees, our hike avoids the toll by parking in a hiker's lot about 100 yards north of the park entrance on CT 85. Walking in on the paved road you pick up a few features that you might otherwise miss. Fields separated by stone walls grace both sides of the entrance road and picnic tables are scattered throughout the area.

You will soon pass an old graveyard on the right—save it for your return. (Note: The trails in Gay City are being redone—this hike has not changed, but the markings have. Trail 8 is now blazed white; at the first junction, the white blazes go left, but you continue straight on the orange trail until it joins the red trail; go left—from here on stay with the red blazes all the way.) Enter the woods on an old road marked Trail 8—a right turn off the road at the western edge of the field.

After .5 mile Trail 9 goes off to the left (it ends at the parking lot near the park's beach). Stay on Trail 8. Just past a small clearing on the right, the old tote road that is Trail 1 crosses your path; go left on Trail 1.

After about another .25 mile you will reach a place where the old road continues past a signpost with no signs; our route goes downhill (the old road continues out of the park) and crosses the Blackledge River on a small footbridge at the site of an old dam. Less than 100 feet beyond the bridge, you hit Trail 7— unmarked at this spot when this was

written—and go left, branching away from the river and proceeding uphill. (If the bridge is out—as it sometimes is in the spring—retrace your steps to the junction with Trail 9 and take that down to the parking lot and Trail 6 and then proceed to Trail 5.) From the top of the rise, take the well-used unmarked trail which goes off to the right. (Trail 7 continues through the break in the old stone wall and drops into a beaver pond.)

Going right downhill you shortly cross a small brook and begin to climb. At the top of the rise, go left on Trail 5, a lovely old woods road. After about .25 mile, cross a brook on a small foot bridge. Trail 6 goes left to the pond, but our hike continues on Trail 5, climbing

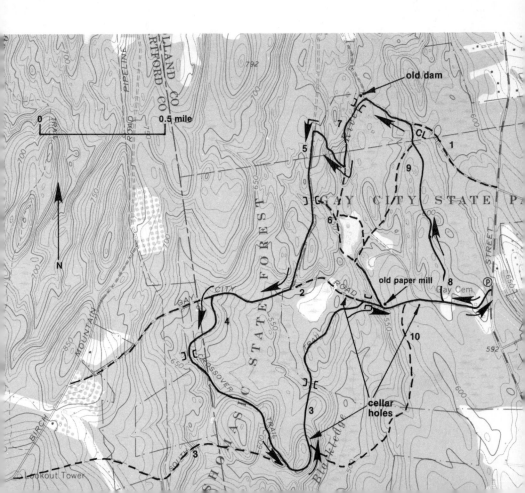

Crossing a bridge at Gay City

gently uphill. Over the rise our route proceeds downhill, shortly joining Trail 2 (North Trail). Go right uphill on Trail 2 (blue blazes). This was the old Gay City Road that was the main route to Glastonbury and the Connecticut River.

The old road climbs gradually. Alert ears may hear occasional noises in the brush; the dash and chirp of the chipmunk, the heavy-bodied bouncing of the grey squirrel, the "scratch-chewink" of the towhee, a common woodland bird with a black back, rufous sides, and a white belly.

Just after crossing a small brook with no bridge, go left on Trail 4 (Crossover Trail). Along this section in the spring you may hear the low-pitched drumming of the male ruffed grouse. He perches on a good log to gives his wings freedom and then beats them faster and faster until his wings become a blur. The resulting thumping attracts females and warns away other males. The first time you hear this sound you may think it is a distant motor running or even wonder if you are really hearing anything at all. We like to think of this soft buffeting as the heartbeat of the New England woods.

In just under a mile you reach the junction with Trail 3 (South Trail). Bear left on the South Trail as you begin the final leg of our circuit. Shortly Trail 10 branches off diagonally back to the right. Continue on Trail 3, where a long boardwalk crosses a swampy area and a brook. The trail then climbs gently to overlook an active beaver pond below you.

Proceed downhill nearly a mile from the crossover junction until you reach Trail 2 on your left and the bridge over the Blackledge River. Just before this junction note the old cellarhole to your left; it is one of many in the park.

Cross the bridge and detour left briefly to view the remnants of the old paper mill. A bit past the old cut stone foundation on your right is a ditch separated from the river by an artificial ridge. The small, now-dry canal diverted water from the pond to power the mill downstream. The pond and the canal assured an even flow; the system dumped out the high water and accumulated water for controlled periods of operation during droughts. In just under .25 mile from the dam the trail drops right off the canal and crosses a bridge over the mill's water sluiceway. The squared blocks of the building's foundation and the square hole that diverted flow from the canal over the waterwheel to the sluiceway are very prominent. The canal was reputed to be ten feet deep in its heyday.

Retrace your steps and proceed left uphill on Trail 2, passing another old cellarhole on your right fronted by four decaying sugar maples. Continue and bear right on the tar road back to your car.

Stop now at the graveyard. It tells a poignant story of the dour little settlement. It is a small plot—a mere dumping ground for the dead. The rival Gays and Sumners are planted on opposite ends of the cemetery. The outlook and character of this vanished town may be reflected in the harsh epitaph on a seven-year-old girl's grave:

"Com pritty youth and see
The place where you will shortly be."

24

Green Falls Pond

Total Distance: 5.7 miles
Time: 3 hours
Rating: CD
Highlights: Ravine, secluded pond, state park
Map: USGS 7½' Voluntown

Far eastern Connecticut seems to have been forgotten by the twentieth century. Roads change from tar to dirt, and stone walls are strikingly square and straight, evidence that they are not the trappings of gentlemen farmers but carefully maintained functional components of working farms. Except for occasional fields and farmhouses, this untenanted, overgrown area is much as the westward-bound pioneers left it. Our hike on the Narragansett Trail to Green Falls Pond takes you through this secluded region.

From the junction of CT 49, CT 138, and CT 165 in Voluntown, drive south on CT 49 for 4.3 miles past dirt Green Falls Road and turn left on Sand Hill Road. In about a mile, turn right onto Wheeler Road—gò .4 mile, where you will see the blue blazes of the Narragansett Trail. Park beyond the blazes, pulling off the road as far as possible; the traffic is minimal.

Enter the woods on the left (east) side of the road by a double blaze on a telephone pole. The trail rolls gently downward with several seasonal streams interrupting the path and soothing the soul with their melodious chatter. This thin-soiled rock-ribbed land is largely clothed in oak.

In .4 mile the trail descends a steep rocky slope toward the valley. It parallels and then crosses a stream. On your left you soon pass a 25-foot rock face graced with lichens, mosses, ferns, and even a few struggling trees. Just beyond is an even more impressive rock face with larger trees growing from its sides. At its base lies a jumble of large rock slabs that were once part of the cliff but have split off since the glaciers bulldozed their way through here. Perhaps these slabs were forced off in years past by trees, since vanished, whose incessant growth slowly but surely split the rock.

After crossing another stream you soon find yourself on the edge of Green Falls River valley by a large crumbling boulder. Look closely at this rock mass; its shade, moisture retention, and slant toward the sun create miniature ecosystems. While the stark, drier sides are grey with lichens, the shaded areas with pockets of soil hold soft cushion mosses. In wet times the surface of a moist, crumbly hollow is colored with light green algae. The thin soil of its horizontal surfaces support clumps of poly-pody fern. Large birches buttress the sides of the boulder which is crowned with an unexpected juniper; the rock's sunny, well-drained top provides the conditions that the juniper needs. An early settler of untended, tired fields, this prickly evergreen is ordinarily shaded out by taller successional trees.

The trail angles left, crossing two rocky seasonal streams. Step carefully, the smooth rocks become very slippery when their covering of mosses and li-chens swells with moisture. After the second stream, proceed gradually uphill and along the valley rim to Green Falls Road, a dirt road 1.4 miles from your start.

Turn right down the road for .1 mile. Turn left off the road and follow the

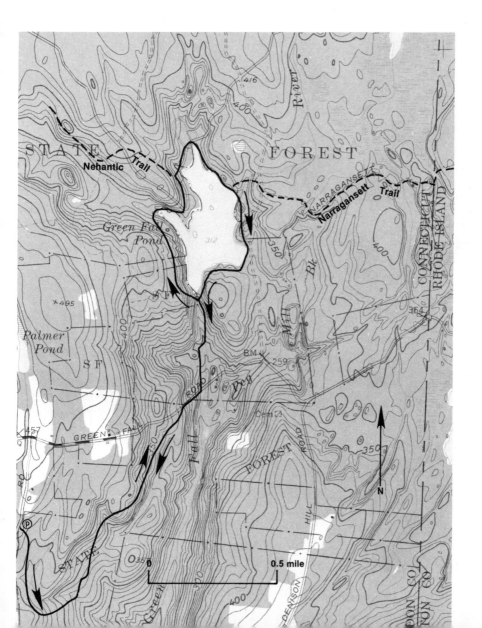

Green Falls Pond

blazed trail along the river, which is now on your right. The path climbs a rocky ridge before slipping down into a narrow ravine which speeds the river over boulders and ledges. About midway to the pond you cross the river at a shallow rocky spot.

The trail clambers over boulders where root-hung hemlocks cling to a steep, eroding slope. The inward-pressing rock walls are thickly covered with mosses and lichens. Soon the trail climbs steadily up the side of the ravine to avoid a sharp drop into the river. Be careful not to trip on the exposed roots along the top.

You reach the base of Green Falls Pond Dam 1.9 miles from the start. The trail crosses the river below the dam almost in the spray of the falls. Climb to the top of the dam. The blue-blazed Narragansett Trail goes right across the dam—we will come back this way.

Go left on the orange-blazed trail around the lake (west) with Green Falls Pond always on your right. This trout-stocked pond is one of Connecticut's nicest—it has lovely ledges dropping into the water, small islands, fully wooded shores, and *no cottages.*

The trail hugs a shore thickly grown with laurel, oak, birch, and hemlock. About .2 mile from the dam the path crosses a feeder stream and continues rounding the pond. If you lose the trail here, head toward the pond—in most places the trail edges the shore. As you advance, picnic tables come into view (many are of massive log construction). A ledge-tipped point to your right is the closest approach to the pond's largest island.

Soon you will reach the gravel road that services the state park—go right. Continue following the orange blazes along the road. There are a few blue blazes scattered along here which should be ignored. Shortly after crossing the major inlet to the pond, the trail turns right. Many of the large outcroppings on your left bear patches of a large, thick-fleshed, curling lichen called rock tripe, which are considered nourishing in case of a dire emergency. Canadian voyageurs reputedly used it to thicken their soups.

The trail is now in sight of the pond. The orange-blazed trail ends at the blue-blazed Narragansett Trail 1.2 miles from the dam; turn right. Cross a small brook on stepping stones; in times of high water an upstream detour will let you cross dryshod.

The trail climbs a rocky ridge for the view of nearby rolling hills, drops down, and visits a rocky point. Enjoy these meanderings—a well laid-out trail lets you explore all points of interest. Go right on an earth-filled auxiliary dam. The underwater face of the dam is covered with rock rip-rap to minimize erosion.

The trail enters the woods just beyond the auxiliary dam. Follow the ridge overlooking the pond before descending diagonally down to the shore. Cross the single handrail dam .7 mile from the end of the orange-blazed trail and retrace your steps down the ravine and back to your starting point.

25

Wolf Den

Total Distance: 5 miles
Time: 2¾ hours
Rating: CD
Highlights: Wolf Den, Indian Chair, state park
Map: USGS 7½' Danielson

Some words roll off the tongue with melodious grace. Although Mashamoquet (mash-muk-it) is definitely not one of those, this state park has a special beauty and grace due to its botanical and zoological diversity. Among the almost infinite attractions of this hike, you will find nestled within the park's 781 acres the legendary wolf den where Israel Putnam, of Revolutionary War fame, reputedly shot the last wolf in Connecticut.

From the junction of CT 101 and US 44 in Pomfret, head south on Wolf Den Drive (shown on the topographical map as Rotham Road) for .7 mile. Turn left into the Wolf Den camping area where there is ample parking.

To reach the blue-blazed trail that loops past the Wolf Den and Indian Chair, walk back down the gravel road and cross Wolf Den Drive. The trail starts by going though an opening in a stone wall where "MASHAMOQUET" has been painted in yellow on a rock. The blazes lead you across an old field before the path turns left into a large stand of smooth alder. Here skunk cabbage spread their large aromatic leaves across the swampy, shaded ground.

Within this thicket the hulk of a great black willow matches its vigor against the dissolution of age.

When you reach the edge of a cornfield, turn left by the shagbark hickory and enter the woods. These first few hundred yards provide a wonderful illustration of the successive stages in the development of a mature forest. You first pass the open field, next the swamp-nurtured invading alder grove, and then cleared wasteland with juniper and red cedar. These trees are among the first to colonize open spaces. The forest is further advanced in the woods just entered; here large red cedars are losing the battle for sunlight to the taller, faster growing birches. In time the birches too will be crowded out by the oaks which comprise the climax forest here. Then fire or lumbering will remove the oaks and succession will start all over again.

Beyond a stream, several large, plate-barked black birches guard the trail, which soon runs parallel to a stone wall. Where the stone wall turns a corner the trail joins a tote road. A red-blazed path goes left cutting across the blue loop trail, but you bear right with the blue

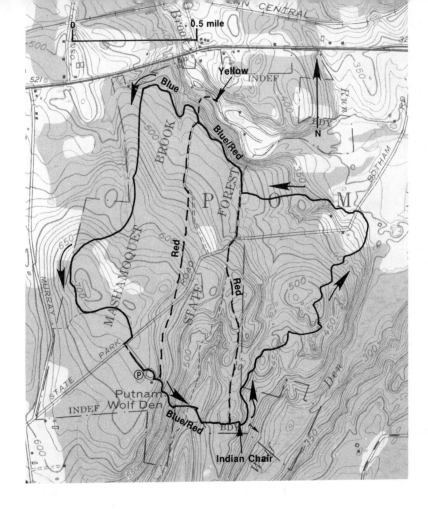

blazes on the level tote road through maturing oak and maple woods. Stay on the blue and red trail (the blazes run together) until the red forks left. (The red trail continues south, crossing Wolf Den Drive—here dirt—and joins our blue trail again just above the Wolf Den.) Follow the blue blazes—shortly a yellow-blazed trail veers right to the picnic and swimming area.

Continuing on the blue trail, your route curves left through the woods, crossing a stream over a new bridge, moves up a gentle slope through large hardwoods, and continues left along an open hayfield. It is easy to let your mind wander as your feet take you down worn old roads such as this one; we still miss marked turns off such an obvious path after thousands of miles of hiking experience.

The trail levels and then meets a gravel road. Turn right and then left almost immediately on another gravel road, passing between a pair of well-built stone cairns. Each cairn contains a large stone with the chiseled words "Wolf Den Entrance" highlighted with yellow paint.

Follow the dirt road back past thick

clumps of laurel to a parking area with a few picnic tables nearby. Continue through the lot to the back of a small circular drive and proceed downhill. Soon the red trail comes in from the left by a vandal-proof cement arrow. The red and blue trails now drop together steeply into the valley below on impressive stone steps. Less than half way down you reach the fabled Wolf Den.

According to legend, it was here in 1742 where Israel Putnam slew the "last" wolf in Connecticut. In fact the last wolf in the state was probably killed near Bridgeport about 1840. Putnam's wolf had preyed on local sheep for some years. Finally after tracking her from the Connecticut River some thirty-five miles to the west, the intrepid Putnam crawled into the den with a lantern, saw the burning eyes of the trapped beast, backed out, grabbed his musket, crawled in again, and fired. Temporarily deafened, he backed out of the smoked-filled hole, paused, went in a third time, and hauled out the carcass.

As you peek inside, note the weathered initials on the sides of the den entrance. In the last century such graffiti was etched on rocks. Today's vandals are lazier—they use paint cans.

When you finish examining the den continue down the slope on the red and blue blazed trail. Cross the brook and climb the sloping ledges on the other side. Just over the crest of the next rounded hill, the red trail breaks off to the left (crossing Wolf Den Drive and rejoining the blue trail where we first met the red blazes in our hike). A short distance beyond, the trail bears left on the slope; here you go right a few feet to a ledge overlook and the Indian Chair. An appropriately shaped boulder, the chair commands a fine view of the surrounding countryside.

Return to the trail and slab left downhill, keeping the stone wall on your right. Shining club moss perches on some of the fern-framed boulders; wood ferns, polypody, and Christmas fern thrive in these shady woods.

Now climb the boulder-strewn hill ahead. The slope is softened near the top by a carpet of white pine needles. After dipping and hesitating slightly, the trail curves right up a rocky draw, turns right, and descends again, passing a black birch and a hemlock embraced in slow-motion mortal combat for the same piece of ground. To your right the evergreen sterile fronds of the maidenhair spleenwort are lodged in cracks of a large seamed boulder. The fertile fronds unfold in spring and die with the first frost.

The trail bends right and then zigzags down the hillside, crossing a stone wall before reaching the field that borders the camping area where you started. Pause to admire the vegetation around the borders of the forest. Nature with all her diversity loves edges. Edges provide habitats for plants that can stand neither full sun nor full shade. Wild animals use the woods for cover and feed on the nearby field plants and border shrubs.

In the nearby woods is a backed-up pond where we flushed a great blue heron. This long-necked bird with a six-foot wing span uses its long legs to keep its plumage above the shallow water he wades in. His sharp-pointed beak unerringly spears small fish, frogs, and other aquatic life that make up his diet. Finally cross the field to your waiting car.

The Indian Chair

Collis P. Huntington State Park

Total Distance: 5.5 miles
Time: 3 hours
Rating: CD
Highlights: Wildlife sculpture, ponds, typical southwest
  Connecticut woodlands
Map: USGS 7½' Botsford

Many of Connecticut's trails are easily found by the casual searcher. Collis P. Huntington State Park in Redding is off the beaten path and frequented primarily by local people. The trails within the park, about 700 acres donated in 1950, are on old woods roads which meander through this secluded area. The land was a gift from Archer Huntington, the stepson of the railroad magnate and philanthropist for whom the area was named. Archer was a noted poet, author, and translator in his own right. Two striking sculptures by the world-renowned Anna Hyatt Huntington (Archer's second wife) adorn this park. Best known for her equestrian statues, it is appropriate that representatives of her wild animal tableaus decorate this park.

To get to this delightful out-of-the-way spot from the junction of CT 302 and CT 58 in Bethel, go south on CT 58 (Putnam Park Road), bear left and then right on Sunset Hill Road. After 2.4 miles on Sunset Hill Road, turn left into Collis P. Huntington State Park. The entrance road is flanked by wildlife tableaus by Anna Hyatt Huntington: wolves baying at the moon at left and a mother bear

with cubs at right. There is a parking lot just inside the gate.

There are no trail blazes to lean on in this park, but the well-trodden paths and woods roads make it relatively easy to follow our route. Go downhill through an open field; then the path narrows and goes down wooden steps to your first junction (you will come back to these steps at the end of the hike). Go right on the well-defined trail through an open area with the too common choking alien — Oriental bittersweet. The animal and bird sounds you often hear here are reminiscent of the background noises of an old jungle movie!

Surrounded by vines, the trail continues downhill bearing left around South Pond. The left trail at the fork allows you to briefly skirt the edge of this pond before rejoining the main trail in a few yards. Shortly a trail heads right, out of the park. Continue straight past a low dam on your left and cross the bridge over the pond's outlet stream. Stay on the well-trodden trail as it curves left around the pond.

After passing a trail on the right you walk through a well-managed woodlot.

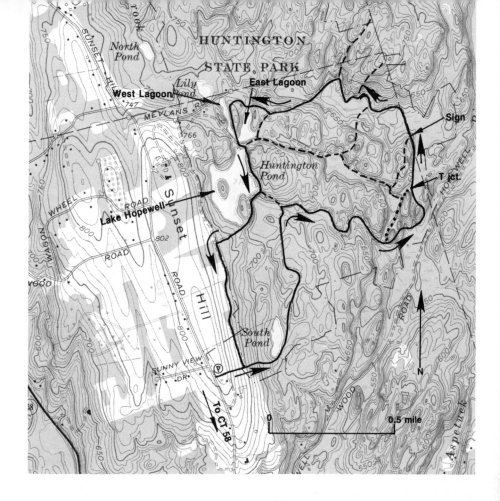

Selective removal has been used to eliminate "junk" species such as black oak and "wolf" trees (oddly shaped trees that have grown in ungainly configurations and do not produce good timber), and to create optimum conditions for the growth of usable trees.

Proceed past the trail at right by a huge split rock. Stay straight on a wide trail, soon passing another trail at right. Pass several scarred beech trees. The beeches' smooth grey bark grows with the tree—it doesn't flake off with time—so marks or initials decades old still retain their shape.

The trail bears right over a small rise. Cross the bridge which spans Lake Hopewell's outlet and immediately go right at the junction which is about 1¼ miles from the start. Soon another trail leaves at left, and also at left there is a grand rock outcropping. A stream comes in and soon parallels the trail on the right.

Shortly reach a "Y" junction below a large rock face—go right. A short side trail leads left to the top of the rock. Our route goes down and then left, reaching a small stream crossing below still more rocks. Cross carefully (no bridge) on an old road and soon you will cross still another stream running under a wooden bridge that is in the last stages of dissolution. Pass through an area of old

Wolves baying at the moon

blowdowns within a narrow stream valley. You can see Newtown Turnpike to the right through the trees in the distance.

The trail parallels the road, climbs uphill, bears left, levels, and crosses a stream on a small footbridge with a large boulder on the right. At the "T" junction go right—there is now a swamp to your right.

The trail now turns left and reaches another junction with a trail sign—go right. After crossing a stream you curve left and then right before reaching still another junction about three miles from the start—stay straight. In about ¼ mile go left at a "Y" junction. Our way curves right and then left uphill to a junction in another 250 yards—go left along the base of an outcropping on your right. Cross the stream—this area has a large number of tulip trees, a more southern tree which is dominant in the Great Smokies National Park.

You climb, then level, passing a stone wall on the right about halfway up the hill. Continue through a rusted gate. Immediately go right on a less used path away from the wide old woods road. (If you wish you may eliminate the loop around East Lagoon by staying on the main trail, which shortly crosses the lagoon's outlet on a wooden bridge and then rejoins our path at the bridge between East Lagoon and Lake Hopewell.)

Parallel a rusted fence, bear right and uphill around East Lagoon. A house soon appears to the right and then West Lagoon can be seen on your right through the laurel. In a short distance you can get a glimpse of East Lagoon (left) again. West Lagoon is still to the right and Lake Hopewell is in the distance dead ahead.

Head down steeply to the shores of West Lagoon and cross between East and West Lagoons on a lovely footbridge. Immediately at the junction go left over still another bridge with East Lagoon at left and Lake Hopewell at right. At the junction just past this bridge go right uphill on a gravel road which goes along and above Lake Hopewell.

At the junction at the lake's end, cross the outlet stream on an earthen dam (at right). At the end of the dam the road curves left. You will shortly see a lightening struck tulip tree. The tree was struck very high and the ribbon of blasted bark can be traced all the way to its base (such bark removal is caused by the instantaneous conversion of the sap to steam which in its violent escape literally blasts off the bark). An extra tall tree such as this gets the lion's share of the life-giving sunlight but because it is the highest point around it is a magnet for lightning bolts.

You parallel a fence, then reach a "T" junction—go left. Shortly you will pass through a gateless pole-flanked opening in the wire fence. Continue on the old road through seemingly impenetrable vine and brush thickets. In about ½ mile you reach the wooden steps (now at right) that you went down a few hours ago. Go back up the steps to your car.

27

McLean Game Refuge

Total Distance: 5 miles
Time: 3 hours
Rating: CD
Highlights: Wildlife, picnic grove, views
Map: USGS 7½' Tariffville

Tucked away in north central Connecticut, the privately endowed McLean Game Refuge was established by George P. McLean, a former governor of Connecticut and U.S. Senator: "I want the game refuge to be a place where trees can grow . . . and animal life can exist unmolested . . . a place where some of the things God made may be seen by those who love them as I loved them. . . ."

Today, be you hiker or cross-country skier, the refuge's excellent trail network provides access to acres of woodlands teeming with wildlife as McLean had hoped. Although it is hard to predict what you will see on any given hike, on a mid-February day we watched a fairly common, but rarely seen, brown creeper moving in fits and starts up a loose-barked hickory, a flock of bustling chickadees, and a chipmunk breaking his hibernation in the above freezing temperatures. A small quick noise proved to be a ruffed grouse taking a few short steps before launching herself with a thunderous roar.

The main entrance to this refuge is located on US 202 (CT 10 in Granby), one mile south of the junction of US 202 and CT 20. Year-round parking is available by a gate at the end of a short gravel road; unauthorized vehicles are not permitted beyond this point.

At the right side of the entrance gate, nearly overwhelmed by faster growing native trees, stands an old apple tree. Such trees are living mementos of the abandoned farms that are scattered through Connecticut's woodlands. The unnatural stretching of its upper branches bears witness to its losing battle for life-bearing sunlight. Spring may bring a few delicate blossoms to this aging specimen; in the fall it yields tart misshapen apples for the deer and the hiker.

Walk along the road a short distance to a three-sided shelter on the left. Here is displayed an inviting map of the refuge's interconnecting trails and wood roads. There are three marked loops — blue, orange, and red — which run together briefly at first. Concentrate on the blue blazes. Cross the bridge over Bissel Brook just beyond the shelter. The loop trails start here on the right.

After ascending a small knoll, look carefully down the slope to the right for two decaying butternut trees. A short-

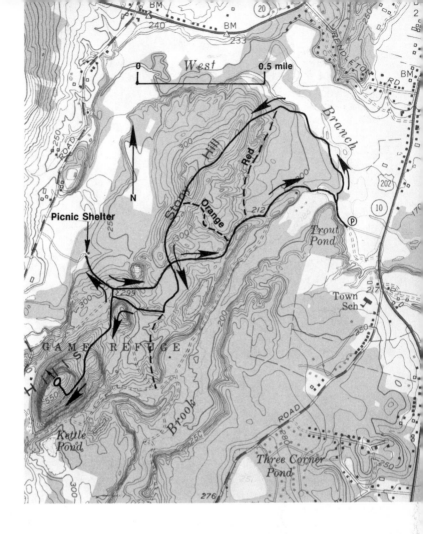

lived member of the walnut family, the butternut tree was used by the early settlers as a source of a yellow water-soluble dye. The nuts have an excellent flavor, but their iron-hard exteriors beneath the sticky green covering are very hard to crack.

The trail which has been following Bissel Brook bends away to the left. About ½ mile from the start at the top of a small rise, the red loop trail leaves to the left (distance around the red loop: 1.25 miles). You should continue following the blue and orange blazes. How-

ever, first look back to the left of the trail and note what's left of the large dead red pine which has several narrow six-inch long vertical holes in its trunk. Only the jackhammer bill of the pileated woodpecker can make such as opening. Although this tree is now dead, newer growth around the hole indicates that the cut was made while this pine was still living. The decayed honey-combed interior indicates that the tree's center had already died and was infested with the fungus-eating large black carpenter ants which are this bird's favorite food.

Canada goose on the loose

After a level stretch, the blue/orange trail tends gently upward. In ½ mile or so you will reach a lovely clearing atop a small rise (Stony Hill) with the Barndoor Hills peeking through the trees to your right. Shortly the orange trail diverges left (distance around the orange loop: 1.5 miles). Keep following the blue-blazed North Trail (now the only blazes you have to contend with) until you reach dirt Mountain Road at 1.5 miles. Here the deep blue blazes of the loop trail go left on the dirt road, but you continue on the lighter (CT Forest & Park) blue blazes. Cross the road and continue on the trail. In .2 mile you reach Summit Trail junction (no sign). After .2 mile more, you come to dirt Mountain Road again.

Going left toward the summit, stay on the blue-blazed woods road. When you reach the top of the rise, watch for the blue-blazed Peak Loop Trail which makes a short right to the top of Barndoor Hill. This is an ideal lunch spot and there are grand views to the north and west. When you have looked your fill, retrace your steps to the signed junction and continue to the picnic grove. At the sign, where the road forks again in about ¼ mile, follow the left branch.

The footpath takes you down a hill to an open hardwood grove with picnic tables, stone fireplaces, and a rustic log cabin which shelters still more picnic tables for the rainy day tramper. (This picnic area may be reached by car from Barndoor Hill Road, a left turn off CT 20, 1 mile west of Granby Center.)

After a second lunch (in case of two views around lunchtime we often save a bit of our lunch for the second location), retrace your steps to the gravel road and turn left to return to the parking area. You cross the trail you walked up, the orange-blazed trail, and the red trail. After .8 mile you pass one of the caretaker cabins.

Just before you reach your starting point the road skirts a small pond. Be sure to save some bread from your lunch to feed the native fish—since fishing is prohibited, they are quite tame. This is an ideal place to identify fish swimming in the water. Watch for the flat ovals of the sunfish and bluegills, the former distinguished by sharper coloration and a sunburst of yellow on their breasts. The vertical barred yellow perch, constantly cruising black bass (with horizontal side stripes), and swarming shiners complete the list of the pond's bread-eating fish. Lurking in the weeds you may see a long thin pickerel sliding in for a quick meal of one of the bread-eaters. This fecund pond is also the annual breeding ground for Canada geese. If you look sharply to the right toward the pond's shallow end, you may notice a large brushpile—a beaver lodge. The beavers occasionally create trouble by damming up the pond's outlet. Continue on the road around the outlet end of the pond to your starting point.

28

Great Hill

Total Distance: 5.5 miles
Time: 3 hours
Rating: C
Highlights: Cobalt mine, cascades
Map: USGS 7½' Middle Haddam

This hike begins on the Shenipsit Trail near a long-abandoned cobalt mine in the obscure town of Cobalt. From there you climb a rocky ridge to Great Hill, which rewards you with a panoramic view over the Connecticut River. A short hike along the ridge brings you to a beautiful secluded cascade at the foot of Bald Hill.

From the junction of CT 66 and CT 151 in Cobalt, drive north on Depot Hill Road. At the first fork keep right up a steep hill. After almost .8 mile, turn right onto Gadpouch Road (no sign in June, 1990), the first right after Stage Coach Run. The blue-blazed trail starts on the left in .5 mile soon after the road becomes dirt. Park on the right nearly opposite the trail head.

Before you start the hike, walk over to a large hemlock grove near your car. The entrance to the cobalt mine (sealed up at the time we wrote this) was down the hill in the shaded ravine. Deep pits on top of the hill tell of the cave-in of the mine roof. Originally opened by Connecticut Governor John Winthrop (son of colonial Massachusetts' John Winthrop) in 1661, the mine was active until the mid-1800s. The cobalt extracted was shipped as far away as England and China for use in the manufacture of a deep blue paint and porcelain glaze.

Return to the trailhead across the road and follow the blazes through ash-dominated hardwoods. These trees range from mature specimens two feet in diameter to fast-growing, strong, light-weight sprouts the size of baseball bats—in fact ash sprouts are used to make all our baseball bats! This section of the trail, always wet and muddy, is at its worst during the spring thaw.

The trail starts climbing gradually. Look to the left for the round-leaved shoots of the wild onion. The leaves and bulb can provide a sharp-tasting treat. In spring, the skunk cabbage raises its hooded head above the soggy ground.

Soon the trail climbs steeply before leveling briefly. When you resume climbing, look to the right for a patch of the creeping evergreen, partridge berry. The tiny heart-shaped leaves set off any of the bright red berries that may have been overlooked by ruffed grouse and white-footed wood mice. Oddly, this relative of the dainty bluet thrives in Mexico and Japan as well as in most of eastern North America.

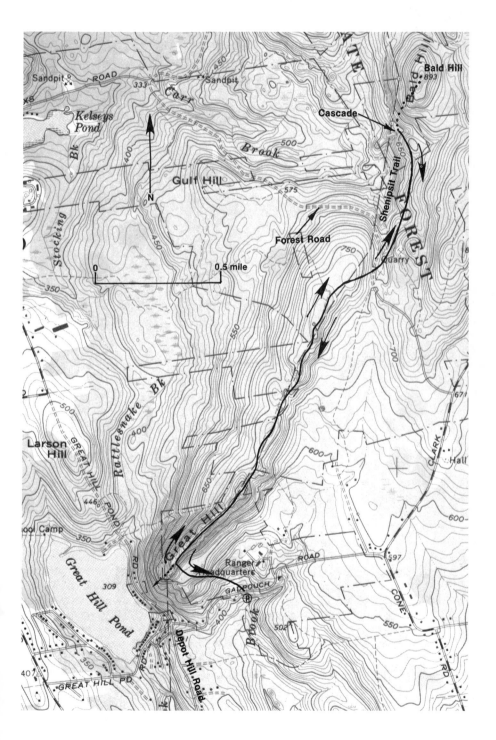

Small cave in Great Hill

The trail zigzags steeply up the rocky side of Great Hill. At the crest take the yellow-blazed trail left a short distance to a rocky lookout. Follow the Connecticut River with your eyes. Directly below you is cottage-rimmed Great Hill Pond. In the middle distance are the smoke stacks of the Middletown power plant. To your left, next to a girder-framed dock, the Pratt and Whitney Middletown Jet Engine facility sprawls over the countryside. At the dock, barges and small tankers offload their cargoes of jet fuel. Continuing southward, the river's wanderings become lost to your eye amidst the horizon's low rolling hills. The Mattabesett Trail follows the western horizon ridges. Northwest of the power plant, the bare slopes of the Powder Ridge Ski area scar the hillside. The old colonial seaport of Middletown lies on the west side of the river.

Retrace your steps to the blue blazes. The trail continues north-northeast along the straight narrow ridge for almost two miles before descending.

About a mile into the hike you'll see several deep holes in a live black oak just to the right of the trail. The pileated woodpecker cut these in his eternal quest for black carpenter ants—if you look closely you will see the remains of the ant galleries at the bottom of some of the holes. By sound and/or smell the birds detect the insects in the rotten heartwood through several inches of living wood and use their great chisel beak to reach them.

About 1½ miles into the hike look for an attractive rock jumble on your right.

Several of the larger flatter rocks have masses of the evergreen polypody fern on them. The deep green leaves of this shade-loving fern arise from creeping rootstocks. It grows on rocks, cliff edges, and even downed trees where acid humus has accumulated. In midsummer the underside of the upper leaflets are decorated with double rows of red brown spore bodies—the next generation.

The trail descends the ridge gradually and joins a tote road 1.77 miles from the start. Used mostly before World War I, tote roads were cut to "tote" logs from the woods. The soil became so compacted from this use that many of these old lanes are still virtually free of vegetation.

After another .2 mile of branching onto several tote roads, the trail crosses a gravel forest road. As you cross to the west-facing slope along this gravel road (Woodchopper Road), notice the scattered, straight, tall tulip trees that were absent from the east-facing slope. Here, near the northern limit of the tulip trees, minor differences of soil or exposure can create distinct demarcation lines. The large tulip-like orange and green flowers and distinctive four-pointed leaves with a notched tip are unmistakable in summer. The numerous flower husks clinging to upper branches make for sure winter identification.

Soon you'll pass the remains of a small quarry and join a relatively recent lumbering road. Continue to follow the blue blazes along this road for about a quarter mile. Now the trail leaves the road and goes left downhill, soon crossing a small brook. After crossing a second, larger brook, the trail reaches a cascade which is at its best during the early spring run-off.

This is a favorite place. In spring the sheet of water flowing evenly down the steep face of the moss-covered rock ledge creates a soothing sound. Bubbles formed in the turbulence glide merrily across the pool at the base of the cascade, accumulating in windrows of pollution-free foam. This is a fine place for a quiet picnic, a good book, or simply a restful interlude.

If you want a bit more exercise (or a more exposed spot to eat your lunch) continue on the blue-blazed trail as it bears right, and climbs nearly a quarter mile to the top of Bald Hill. There are no views here.

When you are ready, retrace your steps, perhaps pausing for a final view from the Great Hill lookout before returning to your car.

Oct 15, 1994
Beautiful sunny day
Exquisite foliage

29

Mount Higby

Total Distance: 5 miles
Time: 3¼ hours
Rating: B
Highlights: Cliff views, volcanic formations
Map: USGS 7½' Middletown

This is a hike that ancient vulcanism built; Mount Higby is a traprock ridge. The rough footing is counterbalanced by sweeping views of the woods, pastoral settings, or superhighways, depending upon where you look.

You start this hike at the junction of CT 66 and CT 147, west of Middletown. Park in the gravel lot well behind Guida's Drive-In. The access trail (blazed blue with a purple dot) starts from the west side of Guida's lot nearly opposite the rear of the drive-in. Reach the blue-blazed Mattabesett Trail after .35 miles and go right. You may want to take a botany detour left to the ditch next to the paved road where you can see some small, pine-like plants. These are horsetails, diminutive descendants of ancient forests. Eons ago they, along with club mosses and ferns, dominated the land, towering over 100 feet high. The silica content of their cells not only betrays their origin in a time when carbon compounds in the soil were far less common than now but suggests their colonial use and name—scouring rush.

Heading back towards Mt. Higby, the trail threads through hemlocks and chestnut oaks parallel to a tote road off

to the right, but you soon cross the tote road and begin to climb the cobbly traprock slopes. After several switchbacks, you finally come out of the stony woods at the open rock Pinnacle, a great viewpoint about a mile from your start. Across CT 66 is Mount Beseck, with Black Pond at its base. Continuing, you hike close to the cliffs with excellent views in a panorama that unfolds as you advance. West Peak and Castle Crag (see Hike 47) are visible in the middle distance; on your right is a traprock quarry. The fields below provide excellent examples of the stages of forest succession: in one field immature evergreen cedars are just rearing above the field's pioneer weeds; in another, mature cedars completely obscure the former pastures; and in still others the succeeding hardwoods are shading out the cedars. Forest succession silently continues.

At your feet along the ridge are large mats of a creeping evergreen shrub: bearberry. The white or pink bell-shaped flowers and tasteless seedy berries are borne in terminal clusters. The Indians smoked the foliage in a mixture with tobacco called by the Algonquin word kinnikinnik (reputed to be the longest single-word palindrome in the English language).

At 1.7 miles the trail drops down into Preston Notch and then climbs a cliff with additional superb views. Along this cliff look for a natural bridge formation with "N.B." painted on it. Scanning the horizon from the summit on a clear day, you will see to the left Long Island Sound and the New Haven skyline. To its left is the long traprock ridge traversed by the vandal-plagued Regicides Trail and the lumpy mass of the Sleeping Giant (see Hike 49). In front of you is an I-91 Interchange; the large building on the right is the University of Connecticut Medical Center in Farmington.

This is also an excellent spot to review visually the northern Mattabesett and southern Metacomet Trails. Ahead, at the end of the ridge you are hiking, the Mattabesett follows a Country Club Road (tar) over I-91, enters the woods and climbs Chauncey Peak (see Hike 36) just beyond the traprock quarry. It continues back along that ridge over Mount Lamentation (partially hidden from view) ending on the Berlin Turnpike (CT 15-US 5).

The Metacomet picks up where the Mattabesett ends, heading west from the Berlin Turnpike over Castle Crag and West Peak (see Hike 47). It then proceeds north on the ridge past the Heublein Tower (see Hike 37) and eventually reaches its terminus on the Massachusetts border at Rising Corners.

Leaving this cliff edge, our trail drops down and then climbs to another viewpoint. On a clear day you can see the Hartford skyline on the right with Mount Tom, north of Springfield, Massachusetts, to the east on the horizon. To the right of Mount Tom the Holyoke Range stretches like a roller coaster—the gap

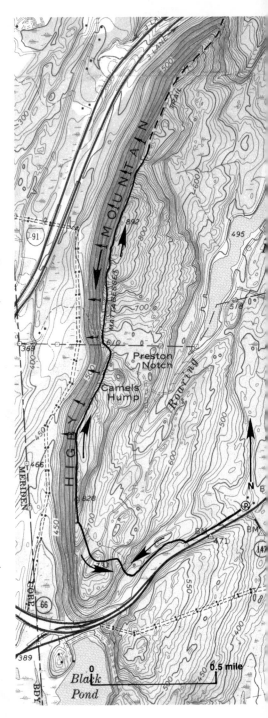

Looking north along the cliffs of Mount Higby

between the two is threaded by the Connecticut River. In the notch between the Holyokes and Mount Norwottuck on the far right, there is a traprock quarry.

At this point take the time to review what you have seen and implant it firmly in your mind; with time these mountains and ridges will become old friends. Have lunch and enjoy the view you have earned. When rested, retrace your steps to your car.

30

Northern Nipmuck

Total Distance: 5¼ miles
Time: 3 hours
Rating: C
Highlights: Wild wooded area
Map: USGS 7½' Westford

The entire 14-mile section of the northern Nipmuck Trail, dedicated in May 1976, offers delightful woods walking. This particular hike offers only four miles of this recent addition to the Connecticut Blue Trail System and makes a loop returning you to your start along two little-used gravel roads with the unusual names of Boston Hollow Road and Axe Factory Road.

The start of this hike is located in northern Connecticut where the crisscross roads are as independent as the people in this area. Follow CT 89 north for four miles from the junction of US 44 and CT 89 in Warrenville. Bear right at the Westford traffic lights. In .3 mile, where the tar road bends right, stay straight on gravel Boston Hollow Road. The blue-blazed trail crosses the road in 1.3 miles. There is enough room for two cars to park on the left.

Follow the blazes north (left) into the woods. In late summer the flat forest floor is liberally decorated with Virginia creeper, wild sarsaparilla, fruiting blue cohosh, plus interrupted and rattlesnake ferns. The latter is the largest and most common of the succulent grape ferns; the simple large triangular leaf and its early season spore stalk are unmistakable.

Shortly the trail climbs steeply onto a hemlock and oak-covered ridge and bears left. Boston Hollow Road, parallel to the trail, is visible below through the trees. Then, winding to the right through thickets of mountain laurel, the path slabs a hemlock-covered hillside. Although the hiker finds mountain laurel lovely—in winter the evergreen leaves add color to the woods and in late spring there is no more beautiful blossom—its tangled growth is the bane of the trail clearer, and it is a tough, stubborn bush whose stubs must be cut off lest they impale the stumbling hiker!

Jouncing up and down several small rocky ridges, you will pass scattered patches of striped maple. Lovely views to the north, west, and south greet you as you reach the top of the ridge before bearing right (west) downhill away from Boston Hollow Road.

If you walk this way in mid-August, you can catch the first signs of the tipping of the year's seasonal hourglass. The lush vegetation looks slightly shopworn. Evergreen plants, previously overshadowed, sparkle with the fresh sheen

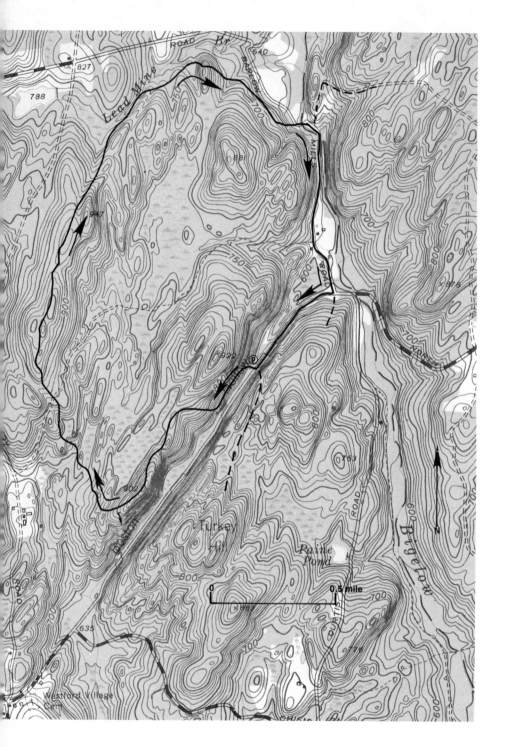

Black-eyed susans at a field's edge

of their new leaves that will carry them through fall, winter, and into the start of yet another spring. Goldenrods and asters—fall's premier flowers—are prominent. The fall's spate of mushrooms has started: white and yellow puffballs, white amanitas that only the real experts dare to sort and eat (the deadliest is appropriately called the destroying angel—it tastes good going down but with the passage of a few hours the now fully absorbed nerve poison is 100% fatal), and the red-capped emetic rusala (also poisonous, but fortunately it can't be kept in the stomach). Moss-bedded dry rocky rills recall spring's long-gone wetness. The ghostly Indian pipes have become blackened skeletons, although they are just erupting through the forest litter in the mountains to our north. Similarly the false hellebore or Indian poke—here quite shriveled—still flowers above treeline in northern New England. An admirer of a particular flower can often prolong the viewing season by moving north with the blooms. In contrast to prolonging the season, if you zig when you should have zagged, you may miss some short-season flower altogether.

In about 2 miles, you cross an old dirt road pointedly labeled "Private Drive" in both directions. Such signs are a reminder that many trails are ours to use only so long as *all* hikers treat the private property that the trails cross with thoughtful care. The uncurtailed vandal can curtail *your* pleasure! After a little ways the trail follows the remnants of an old tote road north, which is soon joined by another tote road coming in from the southeast. The trail then swings right (northwest) off this road. Finally you ascend a hemlock-covered escarpment; below is one of Bigelow Brook's small, noisy tributaries.

In another ½ mile or so, after bearing left downhill, you emerge on gravel Axe Factory Road by a stream-threaded meadow. Although the woods vegetation has faded, late summer brings a riotous flowering in open fields and meadows. Great purple-crowned stalks of Joe-Pye weed, white flowering boneset (an herbal fever remedy), goldenrod, St. Johnswort, the three-leaved hog peanut vine, and pea-like clusters of ground nuts are everywhere. Blackberries invite you to snack, bumblebees engage in a final orgy of nectar gathering, and the sweet smell of pepperbush pervades the air. Here the marshy stream trickles through metal culverts; minnows and pickerel play a deadly game of hide and seek amid the waterweeds.

You are just under 1.25 miles from your car as you come out on the road. Leaving the trail behind, return to your car by following Axe Factory Road to the right and then Boston Hollow Road, also to the right (which goes by your car). Both these gravel roads are little used and a delight to walk. Cement and stone remnants of a mill wall are visible from the next bridge. Pasturing cows and a farm pond farther on compose a peaceful scene—a fitting conclusion to this relaxing hike through the countryside.

31

Natchaug

Total Distance: 6.6 miles
Time: 4 hours
Rating: CD
Highlights: Frog pond, great dead chestnut
Map: USGS 7½' Hampton

Many areas of Connecticut are losing trails because of development, disgruntled landowners, or other conflicting uses, but in eastern Connecticut the trail system is expanding. The greatest growth to date has occurred around the University of Connecticut at Storrs on the Nipmuck and Natchaug Trails. The Nipmuck has been extended 14 miles to Bigelow Hollow State Park near the Massachusetts border (see Hike 30), while an eight-mile addition to the Natchaug Trail now connects to the Nipmuck to form a continuous trail nearly 55 miles long. This hike covers an interesting section of the Natchaug Trail.

From the junction of CT 198 and US 4 in Phoenixville, drive south on CT 198 for .5 mile. Turn sharply left on General Lyons Road; in .1 mile turn right on Pilfershire Road (listed on the map as Pilshire Road) and then turn right again in 1.7 miles on Kingsbury Road where there is a sign to "Unit Headquarters." In about a mile this road becomes dirt. Where the blue-blazed Natchaug Trail crosses, take a gravel road left to Beaver Dam Wildlife Marsh. There is a sizeable parking lot at the end of this road.

The trail curves left and is well-

marked, but the earthen dam backing up the pond to the right is worth a short detour. A stone and concrete apron handles the pond's spring overflow, but the summer stream is usually handled by a vertical corrugated pipe which also acts as a debris screen. The croak-jump-splash of thousands of frogs heralds your approach to the water's edge. In the pond near the far shore is a brush, stick, and mud beaver lodge. You may see beaver cuttings along the start of the trail. The pond surface is almost completely covered in summer with floating and emergent vegetation, especially the rather dull yellow-blossomed bullhead lily and the exotic white-flowered water lily. Tall emergent purple spires of pickerel weed line the shallow shoreline.

Return to the trail which parallels the pond. Several highbush blueberry bushes tempt you to dally and the summer perfume of the pepperbush lightens your way. In the late summer the woodland birds are quiet; they anticipate the coming of fall sooner than we do. Swallows line the telephone wires (they are usually gone by Labor Day) and families of flickers and towhees rummage through the woods together.

After passing through a grove of red spruce and red pine you reach Kingsbury Road in about .6 mile. Follow the road right. There are two kinds of safe three-leaved vines along here; the hog peanut, whose attractive lilac blossoms belie its name, and the virgin's bower

with its fragrant white blossoms. The orange flowers of the aptly named jewelweed, whose foliage is reputed to be a remedy for poison ivy, are common here.

About .8 mile from the start, the trail enters the woods on the left and soon passes through Nathaniel Lyon Memorial Park—named for the first Union General to die in the Civil War. Nathaniel Lyon was born in nearby Eastford, Connecticut. The park features picnic tables, outhouses, a water pump, and a great stone fireplace. Midway across this open area bear left down an old tote road. On this stretch of the trail you wander through mixed hardwood forest, pass occasional stone walls, and finally invade the stillness of a hemlock grove.

In 1.9 miles the erect hulk of a giant chestnut tree, 15½ feet in circumference, commands your attention. It has been dead for 75 years and its seemingly indestructible wood is finally breaking down. In the last few years the main branches have fallen and a portion of the trunk has split away—year by year you will notice more and more of the great tree's dissolution. The photograph was taken in 1977—compare it to the way the chestnut looks now. Except for a few black birches the space around the dead patriarch is respectfully empty. The chestnut sprouts nearby probably sprang from the still-living roots of the dead hulk.

While we were admiring this still-standing relic of our once most valuable hardwood, a small, chunky, brownish grey form circled a stub and disappeared into a knothole. This was only the second nocturnal flying squirrel we have seen in the woods. Its chunky look derives from the folds of skin joining the front and rear legs that allow this little creature to glide (not fly!) from high

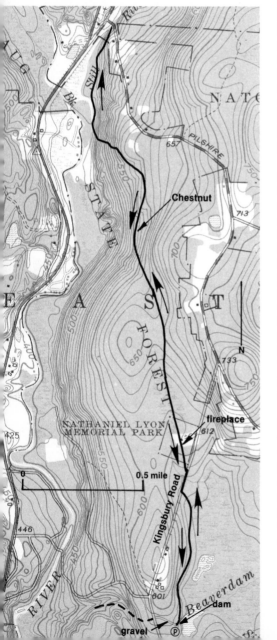

Hulk of a giant chestnut

points to lower locations.

A little further along on the left a much smaller dead chestnut still stands. Identification of dead chestnuts depends upon a rare dissolution sequence—most dead trees rot from the outside in—the chestnut rots from the inside out! The hard intact surface hides a rotting interior. At 2.3 miles you come to a group of circular piles of stones, many perched on large rocks embedded in the ground. In the days of small hand tool harvesters like scythes, this was an efficient method of clearing fields, quicker than building a wall; with today's straight-line mowing machines it would be unacceptable.

Checkered leaves of the evergreen rattlesnake plantain are common along this section of the trail. Its faded spires of last year's orchids thrust upward here and there. This has to be one of the few plants whose foliage is more familiar than its flowers.

In about 2.6 miles turn left down a rutted road. Soon turn right into the woods and bear right again at a wooded grassy remnant of field dotted with red cedars.

Dropping down a bank, you reach and follow the Still River downstream (this trout stream is a tributary of the Natchaug River). In the next ½ mile, you alternately pass through typical woodland and grassy woods featuring the short-lived American hornbeam or musclewood, so-called because its smooth corded appearance is similar to that of a muscular arm contorted with strain. For some reason it does not shade out grass as do most trees.

After 3.3 miles you will reach Pilfershire Road at a bridge. On the upstream corner of the bridge is a large white walnut or butternut—a not too common short-lived tree. Retrace your steps back over the trail.

32

Bullet and High Ledges

Total Distance: 6 miles
Time: 3½ hours
Rating: C
Highlights: Views, interesting stream
Maps: USGS 7½' Voluntown, Ashaway

People talk of the megalopolis extending from north of Boston to south of Washington, D.C., but there is a gap in this urban sprawl. This hike is in the middle of this precious open area. Even as we write, pressure groups, in the name of economics and progress, are trying to run an interstate highway through this land. Hike here and judge the true value of this area for yourself!

The Narragansett Trail to Bullet and High Ledges leads west from CT 49, 4.8 miles south of its junction with CT 138 in Voluntown. Coming from Voluntown, pass Sand Hill Road on your left and then take a sharp right onto the second paved road. Park beyond the stop sign near a formidably-spined honey locust tree.

Here the Narragansett Trail goes along the road and shortly leaves the pavement on a rutted dirt road, flanked by stone walls, to your left. (The paved road curves right to rejoin CT 49, .3 mile north of a striking white-steepled church. The eastern route of the Narragansett Trail heads in here.)

On the right you pass a large sycamore with a massive poison ivy vine climbing on one side. A thick mat of fibrous aerial roots holds it in place. The "shiny leaves three" makes this vine easy to recognize in the summer, but you should become familiar with it in all seasons. The "dormant" winter vine is equally poisonous, especially when the sap courses up the stalks in preparation for spring growth.

The trail continues generally downhill and then levels. In .3 mile turn right off the dirt road (just before a gravel pit), crossing a stone wall. Here the forest floor is carpeted with club mosses: first ground cedar alone (many capped with candelabrum-shaped spore stalks), then mixed with ground pine until finally the ground pine predominates. Past the club mosses, you may find rounded masses of grey-green reindeer moss. The winter mainstay for the caribou herds of the north, this "moss" is in fact a lichen.

The trail rolls with the terrain, crossing and paralleling several stone walls before heading right along a seasonal stream and over another stone wall to Myron Kinney Brook—a river in microcosm. Nature's immutable laws are more easily observed when the familiar is seen on a different scale. Spring runoff

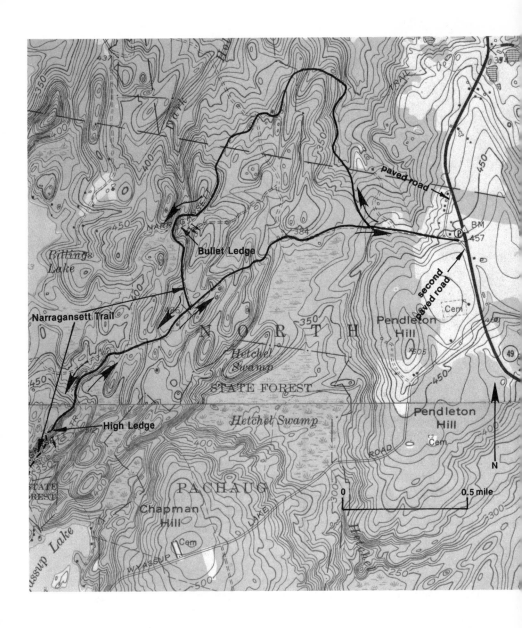

forms the seasonal headwaters of this small brook. Within a few tenths of a mile, small dendritic tributaries entering from both sides swell the brook many times. The water volume increases further from hidden springs where the stream cuts into the permanent water table.

Walk slowly along the stream with an alert eye—the forms darting across gravel riffles and through deep pools are native brook trout. Since these char

Stone wall flanking the Narragansett Trail

need an unending supply of ice-cold water, you will see them in abundance only when you have passed the point where the brook has cut into the permanent water table.

While you are looking for trout, notice how the current rushes around the outer curves of the stream, undermining its banks. Sediment carved from these areas is carried downstream and deposited as sandbars on inside curves where the current is slower.

You leave the brook in about ¼ mile and turn left uphill. The trail then dips to cross a small stream. Fleshy green ribbons cling with numerous short, hair-like roots to the sphagnum moss along the banks. This is liverwort; an evergreen closely related to the mosses, it is one of the most primitive living plants.

Across the stream the trail hugs a stone wall going up the hillside. With posted land on the right and state forest on the left, follow the blue blazes carefully through a network of interlocking stone walls and tote roads.

In an area of prominent ledges, the trail forks left. After ¼ mile merge with an old eroded road. The undulating footpath passes through cozy cornered stone walls and a partially cutover area with mountain laurel stems as thick as a man's arm.

At one point the old road that you are on crosses another road (you continue straight ahead). If you do detour right a bit on this second road you will see at least two alien flowers—day lily and gill-over-the-ground—a sure sign that an old homestead existed here.

The trail continues generally upward with a rocky ridge to your right. When the trail takes a steep turn downward, continue instead straight ahead to the Bullet Ledge Lookout. Step carefully— copperheads are sometimes found here.

Return to the trail and descend steeply to the rocky valley floor. When you reach the tote road set between a rock ridge and a swamp, turn left. Following the blue blazes at succeeding junctions, you finally emerge on a deeply rutted old town road flanked by stone walls. To the left, this road leads back to CT 49. Generally when you find an abandoned road with stone walls on either side, it means that this was an old main town road leading from one place to another rather than a wood-gathering tote road that goes nowhere.

Turn right on this old road for the climb to High Ledge. Fork left off the road at the trail sign giving the distances to High Ledge (.7 mile), Wyassup Lake, and Lantern Hill.

The trail climbs onto an oak and hemlock ridge. After about .5 mile it dips slightly into the valley before quickly rising to the edge of a steep hill. You wind through ledges before dropping into a narrow, rocky valley. Cross the stream and climb steeply, bearing left toward High Ledge.

A rocky point perched above the valley, High Ledge affords a bird's-eye view of nearby treetops. Island-dotted Wyassup Lake sparkles in the middle distance. On a clear day the faint line of Long Island Sound can be seen beyond the lake against the horizon. On the right you can pick out the fire tower on Wyassup Lake Road.

If you wish to hike 7 miles, just retrace your steps to your car. The alternate route along the rutted old town road (mentioned earlier) to CT 49 shortens the distance by one mile.

33

Westwoods

Total Distance: 6 miles
Time: 3½ hours
Rating: CD
Highlights: Rocks, ledges, salt water.
Map: USGS 7½' Guilford

This 2,000-acre open space in Guilford is an attractive woodland with a touch of salt. The lake at the far end is brackish, and as you hike the labyrinth of trails gulls wheel overhead. Because it is so near to Connecticut's overdeveloped coast, Westwoods is especially prized.

From the junction of US 1 and CT 77 in Guilford proceed west on US 1 for .7 mile. When you reach Bishop's Apples on the right, turn left onto Peddler's Road. In one mile, reach a small parking area on the left at Trail Entrance #2: Peddler's Road. The white circle trail starts here.

Westwoods, like Sleeping Giant (see Hike 49), has an extensive trail system. On the hike described here, follow the white circle trail out and the orange circle trail back. In the interest of clarity and brevity, we won't mention most of the numerous other trails you cross; directions to other routes in Westwoods are available in the *Connecticut Walk Book*. In general, however, the trails blazed with painted circles run north-south and those with painted squares east-west. Mosquito repellent is a must on this hike in the summer. Along the shore, because of extensive marshy breeding grounds, these pests always seem bigger, bolder, and more numerous than elsewhere.

The white circle trail goes along the left side of the entrance road, crosses an open area, and goes uphill very briefly before bearing right and heading downhill. Pass the green trail on left and continue on the white circles. Shortly our trail goes left downhill as the white squares continue straight ahead—stay on the white circles. In late May your way is strewn with the white petals of flowering dogwood—nature's confetti.

Shortly you will reach the Great Marsh plank walk. Cross slowly enough to appreciate the rich diversity of plants but quickly enough to avoid being eaten alive! At the start you see the deeply notched, paired, short-stemmed leaves of the arrowwood, the wedge-shaped leaves of the coastal pepperbush, the broad leaves of the skunk cabbage, and the large, multi-cut leaves of the cinnamon fern encircling its large cinnamon-colored fertile fronds. Bunched tussocks of sedges ride the muddy area, the old dead leaves and roots forming the clump from which the new razor-sharp grasslike leaves sprout.

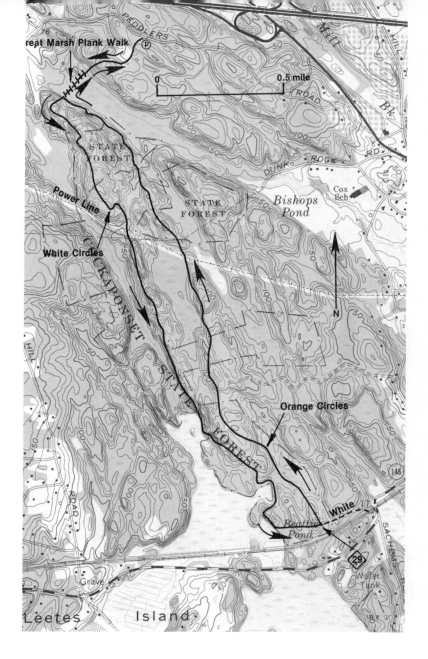

Leaving the plank bridge at the junction of the orange, yellow, and white trails, stay on the white circle trail, and rise into a dry, thin-soiled area covered with laurel and hemlock. In general, the trails flirt with a multitude of rocks, ledges, and glacially rounded outcroppings; they were laid out with much thought and care. The terrain that made Westwoods a farmer's wasteland has given birth to a hiker's wonderland.

Stay on the white circle trail as it

On the Great Marsh Plank Walk

twists and turns, climbing to broad rock outcroppings and descending to the floor below again and again. Soon after passing junction 22, the white square alternative loop goes on a wonderful rock adventure rejoining the white circle trail on the other side of this rock jumble. Continue to follow the white circle trail's gyrations.

About one mile from the start you

pass under a power line. Pink ladyslippers grace the trailside and are scattered throughout the undergrowth. We have even heard that the elusive yellow ladyslipper has been found in Westwoods. If you listen carefully you may pick out the szweet-szweet-chur-chur-chur of the cardinal—in wintertime the brilliant red of this bird against the snow is especially striking. This bird has become common in Connecticut only in the last few decades. Possible explanations of this northward expansion of its range include climactic change, extensive artificial winter feeding, and response to agricultural change.

The white circle trail continues over and around rocks, finally going through a great rock cleft for nearly 25 yards. After some two miles of walking you will catch your first glimpse of brackish Lost Lake from a ledge overlook. You actually reach the phragmite-bordered shores in another half mile, and then climb to a final ledge which offers good views off the trail to the right. Since this spot is about halfway through the hike, it makes a good lunch stop.

Leaving the lake, watch for the old quarry on the right where the trail curves left. Broken slabs with drill-marked edges lie between it and the trail. Look carefully, you may be able to pick out examples of stonecutters' whimsy—scalloped rocks, hollowed out boulders, and the like, that were probably etched in idle moments.

You soon reach junction 29 in about three miles. All major junctions are numbered with signs placed high in the trees to minimize the effects of souvenir-hunting vandals—the worst kind for hiking trails. Keyed to the park's map, which is found in the *Connecticut Walk Book*, these numbers enable you to place yourself exactly.

Turn sharply left onto the orange circle trail; shortly you pass through a hemlock grove so thick no undergrowth exists, a sharp contrast to the lush wood you hiked through earlier. The combination of leafy sun-screening branches and thick tannin-rich needles on the forest floor serves to exclude all plant life from this understory.

Cross a wood bridge and bear left; shortly cross another bridge, then another brook; continue on the orange circles. Pursuing this route, you will come to the base of a very large overhang—the so-called Indian Caves—one of at least a thousand so named in the state!

Pass beneath the power line again at about five miles and soon come to junction 14. Continue on the orange circles as you overlook a small pond and proceed along the base of yet another cliff and through a rock jumble. You soon come to another overhang (another Indian Cave?) beside a marsh. Shortly reach the junction with the white circle and yellow trails at the Great Marsh plank walk. Cross the marsh on these convenient planks and return to your car.

34

Oct. 22, 1994
3 hrs 15 minutes
Finished around 5:30 PM
One snake plots of climbers
Referred hikers to Rogers Orchard
and saw them there.

Ragged Mountain Loop

Total Distance: 6 miles
Time: 3½ hours
Rating: CB
Highlights: Views, rock climbing
Maps: USGS 7½' New Britain, Meriden

Rock climbing is a sport for methodical people who wish to place themselves in careful jeopardy. Perhaps the urge to rock climb is innate, but the skills must be learned and learned well! Every year several neophytes take the rock climbing course offered by the Connecticut Chapter of the Appalachian Mountain Club. Only a few graduate, but they are usually hooked for life.

The Ragged Mountain Loop passes the premier rock-climbing area in Connecticut (consult *Traprock* by Ken Nichols, published by the American Alpine Club) and the place where the course for beginners is given. You may see them in action and marvel at their daring exploits on these cliffs.

To get to this area of volcanic cliffs, start from the junction of CT 372 and CT 72 in New Britain. Take CT 372 (Corbin Avenue) east for 1.6 miles to its junction with CT 71A (Chamberlain Highway). Take this for 1.3 miles to a right turn onto West Lane. Proceed on West Lane for .6 mile to Ragged Mountain Memorial Preserve (563 acres). The topographic map was photorevised in 1972. Since then the route numbers have been changed, e.g. Corbin Ave was CT

72, and is now CT 372, and CT 72 is a superhighway.

Follow the blue blazes with red dots about 100 yards to the beginning of the loop proper. We will go out on the left arm of the loop and return on the right.

Immediately the trail bears left off the woods road. (Be careful—it is very easy to continue blithely along a well-defined woods road and miss where the trail turns off. We have done it many times.) The trail bears left yet again away from the well-worn path, which continues straight. Climb gently on the trail, which is well marked with blue/red blazes. The trail soon levels and goes due south, then continues climbing, passing an old woods road on the right, and then leveling yet again.

The Connecticut woodlands are crisscrossed with innumerable woods roads; some are easily followed, some have become choked with brush, and some are so faint as to defy certain identification. These roads were cut and used (usually just a short time) to harvest the wood and/or charcoal that were major products of our woodlands in the last couple of centuries. The disused roads are slowly but surely being obliterated

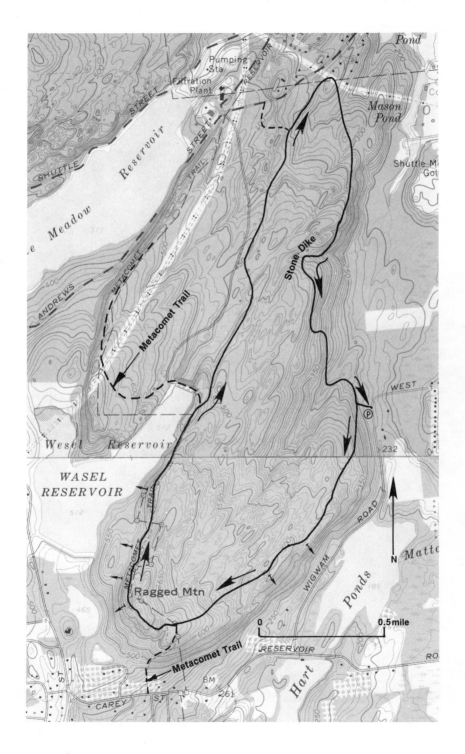

The top of Ragged Mountain cliffs

by the healing hand of nature.

Just as our path (another old woods road) begins to drop, the blue/red blazed trail we are following takes a sharp right, soon crossing yet another old woods road. The trail loops back to the woods road and then leaves it again at left. Our trail climbs to a rocky ridge where Harts Ponds are visible through the trees. Continue on the ridge, soon climbing to an excellent lookout above the ponds.

The ridge-top trail goes down and then up, soon leveling and then reaching another fine viewpoint above Reservoir Road. Continue on open ledges with fine views to the south where Castle Crag and West Peak (Hike 47) can be seen in the distance. (West Peak is one of the highest volcanic rock spots in Connecticut.)

The trail drops into and then out of another small ravine. Permanent water is rare in traprock—snow melt and rain soon run off this impervious rock, leaving most ravines stark and dry. Continuing south along a small rock ridge, the trail then turns down and left off the end of the ridge before climbing again to more views and a free-standing wall— difficult to describe but you will know it when you see it—1.2 miles from the start. The tops of Central Connecticut's traprock ridges provide good, development-free hiking with excellent views.

After 1.7 miles the blue/red-blazed trail reaches the blue-blazed Metacomet Trail at the top of Ragged Mountain. We will follow the Metacomet Trail for the next 1.4 miles before looping back to the car. Proceed north on the blue-blazed trail. After one more dip and steep climb, you reach the top of the Ragged Mountain Cliffs, which here are largely wooded. In about another half-mile of gentle ups and downs you will come out into the open. Here, of necessity, many of the blue blazes are painted on rocks instead of on trees.

We sat atop the cliffs and watched three sea gulls play "follow-the-leader" above the reservoir. Large birds often use the thermals associated with cliffs to soar for hours with nary a wingbeat. To the north, the University of Connecticut's Medical Center in Farmington is usually visible even on hazy days. Far below you can see strollers sauntering along the reservoir dike.

The trail bears right away from the cliffs, drops down and rises up again as it undulates along the ridge. A final lookout offers views of the north end of Wasel Reservoir.

Volcanic ridgetops are not usually good places to find large varieties of flowers, but we have found one especially favorite flower in traprock locations in Connecticut (but rarely elsewhere): pale corydalis, a member of the poppy family, closely related to bleeding hearts and Dutchman's breeches. Whenever you traverse these ridges be on the lookout for this striking rose and yellow flower.

The trail then wends its way towards the reservoir shore. The trail surface requires proper hiking footgear— not street shoes. Near the end of the reservoir on an open rocky ledge we leave the blue-blazed Metacomet Trail and turn right on the blue/red Ragged Mountain Loop at a well-signed junction. Follow the well-marked trail, eventually reaching a deeply eroded woods road (constant cutting of the soil with wagon wheels combined with a slope and water run-off created this erosion—today's trail bikes which too often illegally use our trails do the same thing). Then at the brook crossing, the feeder trail to Shuttle Meadow Avenue goes left. Go right to West Lane (very well-signed).

After about one mile our trail turns sharply right and climbs alongside a small stream (crossing it once) to a lovely waterfall. Here you will find the remnants of a stone dike. Climb carefully up the loose traprock slope to the ridgetop and turn left as the trail continues south. Here, though the trail is not well-worn, it is well-blazed. The trail descends, goes along the hillside, and descends again. Shortly you cross a deeply eroded old road, then a brook, and then descend gradually to an old woods road.

Go right about .1 mile to reach the beginning of the loop you started a few hours ago. At the junction go left to your car.

All-Day Hikes

35

Devil's Hopyard

Total Distance: 4 or 7.5 miles
Time: 2½ or 4½ hours
Rating: CB
Highlights: Cascades, falls, impressive trees, views
Map: USGS 7½' Hamburg

Water dominates the 860 acres of Devil's Hopyard State Park; water in the form of rushing, turbulent Eight Mile River and its tributaries; water as the agent that gave shape to this rugged scenic area.

Throughout this state park, you pass beneath groves of great trees, primarily hemlock, with wide boles, straight trunks, and first limbs often twenty feet or more above the ground. They create a brush-free setting for your explorations. The main hike is presented as the spectacular falls and giant trees that most come to see, but we have added a loop on the other side of the road that, while less spectacular, lets you stretch your legs quite a bit more.

The Devil's Hopyard became a state park in 1919 and is fully developed, with picnic tables, fireplaces, rainy weather shelters, campground, and several miles of hiking trails. The origin of its colorful name is lost in a welter of fanciful stories ranging from the simple corruption of Mr. Dibble's hopyard to tales of mist-shrouded forms seen dancing on the ledges amid the spray of the falls.

From the junction of CT 82 and CT 156 in East Haddam, drive east .1 mile on CT 82 to Hopyard Road. (The road sign was down when we scouted this hike, but there was a brown state park sign designating Devil's Hopyard Park.) Turn left (north); follow this road about three miles past the park entrance and turn right on unsigned Foxtown Road. Park in the small paved lot on your left just before the bridge. The campground is just beyond the pond on the left.

Cross the road and go down the trail past the covered bulletin board. Shortly you will pass the dark red-blazed Millington Trail at right—we'll explore this trail on the way back. Continue down past Chapman Falls. For over a century prior to its inclusion in the state park, this sixty-foot waterfall powered a mill (remains of mills and mill dams abound in New England). The sheets of water now fall freely in a series of falls and cascades. To get the full impact of these falls you should view them both from above and below. The rocks beside the trail have many circular holes and a smooth dry chute where the water used to go. The holes were formed when a hard loose rock got caught in a small indentation in the ledge. The force of the

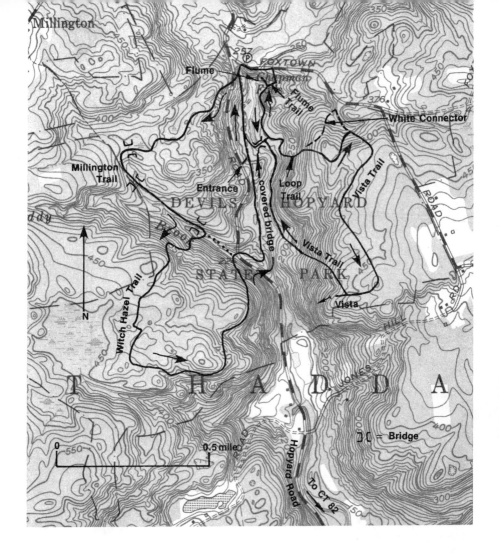

flowing water caused this rock to gyrate in the cavity, eventually wearing a circular hole. After the first rock is worn away, often another one falls in to continue the erosion.

Stop a moment to consider the "why" of a waterfall. You need a special condition of a harder rock overlaying a softer rock so that the under layer will erode at least as fast as the more greatly stressed upper layer. If these conditions do not exist a waterfall will become a series of rapids or cascades which ef-

fectively move the water down from a higher to a lower area, although not as dramatically.

You soon join the park road and continue below the picnic shelter to the covered footbridge. Cross the river (liberally stocked with trout) through the covered bridge and immediately turn left and follow the orange blazes along the riverbank to the Flume, a dry water chute.

From here you can see both Chapman Falls on the left and a series of lesser unnamed falls on the right. For a

View to Eight Mile River Valley

look at the lesser falls, cross a small bridge over a tributary stream. Now retrace your steps to the covered bridge and continue on the orange Vista Trail until at the junction you turn left on the blue-blazed Loop Trail. When the trail forks, bear right and continue to the upper junction with the orange-blazed Vista Trail. Now follow the orange blazes towards the Vista.

Notice the clear brown color of the brook on the right. This discoloration is not caused by pollution but is the result of tannin in its water—probably leached from the hemlocks which dominate the park.

At the top of the hill, you join a well-worn path that was part of an earlier trail system. Soon an arrow directs you to cross the brook on a series of stepping stones. Continue uphill (with the brook on your left) on the orange-blazed Vista Trail. This trail levels briefly and then continues down a sloping plateau.

Soon you pass a huge white oak with pocked, unhealthy-appearing bark. The tree is in the last stages of normal dissolution (however, with oaks this disintegration can take decades!). One whole side has split off (lightning?), exposing an enormous decaying scar. Great bands of rounded new growth flank the gash; in vain, this great oak has tried to cover its decaying heartwood, now freckled with fruiting fungal bodies and riddled with dry rot. Most of its great limbs have fallen; a few green leaves are its only sign of life. The surrounding thick stand of young hemlocks is the forest's response to the flood of sunlight released by the dying patriarch.

After crossing a seasonal stream, the trail bears left uphill, levels, and crosses another small stream. Continue on this level trail until you come to a large hemlock blazed with an orange arrow directing you to the right. Proceed downhill,

following the orange blazes to the vista. You soon reach a footpath that breaks to the left off the main trail. Follow this path downhill for about 150 yards to a rocky outcropping on the edge of a steep drop.

The Eight Mile River valley lies below you. Hemlocks march down the steep hillsides. The dammed remains of a pond form the centerpiece of your view; directly beyond, a single farm and field breaks the undulating blanket of treetops. A closer look shows that the field is an alluvial fan. Eroding water tore this material from the hills behind it and when the current slowed dropped this debris in a fan-shaped area, flattening the valley floor and creating an optimal area for farming.

After enjoying the vista, retrace your steps to the main trail, watching carefully for the junction, and head left downhill. Our orange-blazed trail bears right toward the river and follows it upstream. After a bit, the trail bears slightly right, away from the river, and ascends a stepped ledge to a hemlock-covered flat. It then runs gently down to the covered footbridge, passing the blue Loop Trail at right on the way.

Cross the bridge and go right up the road towards the parking lot where you left your car. Now you may choose to return to your car, having done the four-mile loop, or follow our directions to add another 3.5 miles to your day.

To continue your hike, take the red-blazed Millington Trail (now on your left). Follow the red blazes as the trail continues just below and then crosses the road. The well-used foot trail continues diagonally left, slabbing gently up the hill. Before reaching the top, however, a sign directs you left off the eroded way. Once up the hill, the red-blazed trail undulates across the top through a largely oak and hickory forest.

Shortly after passing some angular boulders you come to a sturdy wooden bridge built by a YCC team in 1978 that crosses the stream you have been hearing. Then you cross a swampy swale on a very small wooden footbridge and reach an old woods road. A red blaze on a tulip tree tells you to go left. Your footpath here slopes gently downhill with the sound of running water on your left.

The trail crosses the stream again on another YCC-built bridge. This flowing water first takes the form of cascades and then miniature falls. After this the sound of water is on your right.

In a cooling grove of hemlocks, cross the steadily growing stream yet again on a third YCC-built bridge. Immediately on the other side of this third bridge a yellow-blazed trail cuts in — go right on it uphill away from the well-worn path. This route soon reaches Baby Falls, which are on the right and down a steep hill. Sit a while on an aging wooden bench to enjoy this example of waterpower in miniature.

When ready, continue following the yellow blazes uphill. You are now on the Witch Hazel Trail, which soon steepens and moves away from the stream, then levels across the top, passing through an area lush with ferns: Christmas, cinnamon, beech, and New York. The woods here are a mixture of oak, northern birch, and hickory.

The trail turns downward; at one point you pass under a canopy of ancient mountain laurel bushes. The tops are ten to fifteen feet above you, supported by boles almost as thick as your leg.

Finally your route makes a steep descent through a thick grove of hemlocks. Note the almost total lack of undergrowth where these trees grow thickest. The hemlock's thick shade and the strong tannin from several years accumulation of fallen needles and other debris prevent most plants from gaining a foothold, creating practically a monocultural grove.

Just as you emerge from the woods you join the dark red blazes that you left a mile or so back. Both the dark red and yellow loops come out together on this woods road.

Cross the tar Hopyard Road and proceed down the now dark red-blazed trail (the yellow blazes ended at the tar road). Pass through another grove of hemlocks. The trail joins an old tote road. You will soon see the Eight Mile River on your right. Picnic tables are scattered among the trees.

You come again to the "small" stream that you have crossed so many times. Now it is large enough that you may be glad to see the small footbridge a few yards down the stream. The trail leads left and joins another tote road.

After climbing a hill, you will see a rock wall on your left — this supports the tar entrance road. The trail now follows a rough gravel road parallel to the tar road. You soon reach the tar park road that services the main part of the park. Follow this right past several small parking lots and up the hill to your car.

Chauncey Peak and Mount Lamentation

Total Distance: 6 miles
Time: 4 hours
Rating: B
Highlights: Superb views
Map: USGS 7½' Meriden

The traprock ridges within the Connecticut River Valley are a hiker's paradise. Ascents are steep and rugged, but the views from the cliff edges are superb. This hike along a section of the Mattabesett Trail has some of our best traprock cliffs and offers a panoramic view within the first .5 mile. Climb Chauncey Peak and Mount Lamentation on a cool clear day and you won't be disappointed.

From I-91 near Meriden, take exit 20 to Country Club Road. Follow this road west about 3 miles. Since Country Club Road connects the trails on Mount Higby (see Hike 29) and Chauncey Peak, blue blazes appear occasionally on telephone poles along the way. Where the road makes a sharp left turn, continue straight into the parking lot at Bradley Hubbard Reservoir. The blue-blazed Mattabesett Trail runs just below the dam at right and continues up the hill and around to the right before joining the old trail below Chauncey Peak.

As you rejoin the old trail, you pass a large bed of gill-over-the-ground, a small member of the mint family with tiny blue tubular flowers. This alien was once used to ferment beer. Shortly you come across patches of wild onion—a strong flavor for your sandwiches—and silverweed. Gerry first identified silverweed, which looks like a many-leaved strawberry plant, in Newfoundland, and we've since spotted it several times in Connecticut. This illustrates one of the values of recognition; once you've identified a plant, you will notice it where you never realized it existed.

The trail soon starts to climb, becoming steadily steeper and rockier. Many flowering dogwoods light the forest's middle story along the way. After hiking about ½ mile, you finally pass through almost sheer traprock ramparts and emerge on the level top of Chauncey Peak (688 feet). The southern panorama you see is very special.

New Haven and the faint blue line of Long Island Sound lie straight ahead to the south. The lumpy mass to the right is the Sleeping Giant (see Hike 49) and then West Rock ridge. Directly right stretch the Hanging Hills of Meriden; South Mountain partially blocks Castle Crag and West Peak (see Hike 47). To your left rise the cliffs of Mount Higby (see Hike 29).

All these ridges and related formations

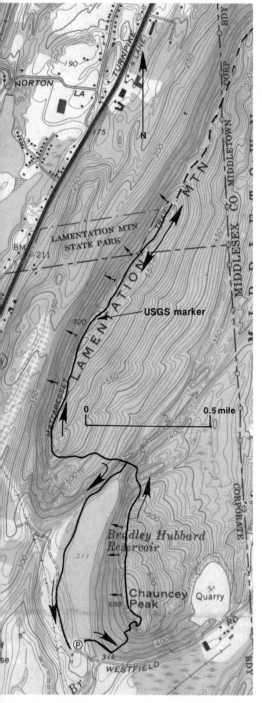

are composed of traprock formed some 200 million years ago when this land was volcanically active and the great crack that eventually became the Atlantic Ocean was expanding. Most are remnants of vast upended lava sheets, but a few, like West Rock ridge, are exposed lava dikes.

The trail tacks east along the southern cliff edge and then turns left to meander across the top to the western cliffs. The trees you pass on top are predominantly chestnut oak and staghorn sumac, two species that can tolerate this thin dry soil. As you reach the edge, the view south looks down on a traprock quarry (this hard stone when crushed is an ideal highway base). Unfortunately, a little farther on, the quarry has expanded to eat away the mountain.

The vistas from these cliffs are among the finest in the state; as you work your way along the edge, rocky outcroppings provide unobstructed views of Crescent Lake (Bradley Hubbard Reservoir) 400 feet directly beneath you. From the final outcrop, the vista sweeps from New Haven west past the Hanging Hills and north past the Hartford skyline to the hills crossed by the northern section of the Shenipsit Trail (see Hike 18).

The trail drops off Chauncey Peak, crosses an old canal about .8 mile from the start, and heads up a wide rocky path. Following the blue blazes, bear left at the fork and left again when you reach a tote road. In a few yards the blazes lead to the right back into the woods. Climbing steadily uphill, you curve around the southern end of Mount Lamentation (720 feet) and emerge on the western cliffs of this ridge 1.8 miles from the start. The trail passes a USGS bench marker at 2.1 miles.

While taking an unmarked detour through the woods here we came across a fearless black rat snake. This one was 4½ feet long—average for this species (they grow to 6 feet). Unfortunately, these rodent-eating snakes are too easily killed by vandals. This one let Gerry gently lift it off the ground so we could see the underside checkerboard pattern that distinguishes it from the similar but more common black racer. How easily a misguided person could have killed it!

The trail parallels the cliffs for another mile and ends with a particularly fine view that extends from New Haven to Hartford and beyond. On a clear day you can identify the traprock ridges north of Springfield, Massachusetts. From left to right, the east-facing cliffs of Mount Tom are followed by the gap cut by the Connecticut River, the multi-summited Holyoke Range, and finally Mount Norwottuck. This last peak marks where the emergent traprock disappears into the valley's older red sandstone.

You may simply retrace your steps to your car or follow the alternate route (which we recommend): retrace your steps to the point where the trail reaches the rocky old tote road. Instead of following the road left with the blazes, go right downhill. Soon you reach the shore of Crescent Lake (Bradley Hubbard Reservoir). Continue on the unmarked trail that hugs the shore. Across the lake above you are the cliffs you traversed earlier. Soon the path hits an old road—continue on this road along the lake. At the fork (power lines are visible about 200 yards away at right), follow the trail left along the shore through the tall, straight, red pines. At the end of the lake, you emerge into the small parking lot where you left your car.

Almost there—Chauncey Peak

37

Heublein Tower

Total Distance: 7 miles
Time: 4 hours
Rating: C
Highlights: Scenic reservoir, views, tower
Map: USGS 7½' Avon

Close by the city of Hartford is a large attractive area of open reservoir land. Preserved to maintain water purity, areas such as this one in West Hartford are often open to non-polluting activities. A nice day brings out an endless procession of walkers, joggers, bicyclists, hikers, and—in winter—ski tourers. The value of this land is incalculable.

From the junction of US 44 and CT 10 in Avon, proceed east for 2.3 miles. On the left (north), a sign indicates Reservoir 6, Metropolitan District. Turn in here; there is ample parking.

Walk to the far end of the parking lot and bear left on the dirt road that is barred to motor vehicles. This becomes the blue-blazed Metacomet Trail. Along your route are great rhubarb-like leaves of the burdock; their nondescript flowers yield the round, multi-hooked burrs that dogs and hikers pick up in the fall. These plants usually grow alongside trails and in front of camping lean-tos because when hikers stop and remove them from their socks or pants they throw the burrs or seeds down where they are. The fresh green growth of grapevines edge out into the dirt road where they are soon beaten back by the pounding feet of joggers. Shaded by hemlock, spruce, and pine, this west shore of the reservoir is lovely any time of the year.

The wind-stirred wavelets on the reservoir reflect the sun in a sparkling glitter that adds life to this shifting scene. Along the shallow edges of the water swim numerous species of the sunfish family (including the black bass); this border area provides protection from predators and is handy for snaring land-based insect life.

The shiny-leafed vine on the reservoir side of the cement bridge is the harmless five-leaved Virginia creeper, but the small cement and stone bridge abutment used to be covered with great masses of poison ivy. In the spring of 1983 you could still see remnants of these vines with their numerous root hairs embedded in the cement (the root hairs are a giveaway when identifying poison ivy). There is still much poison ivy along the way and nestled within its foliage you may find its lovely greenish-yellow blossoms. Along here we saw a pair of four-foot black rat snakes. Very effective rodent eaters, they are now considered a threatened species by the

Connecticut Herpetological Society. As with many of our larger creatures, its major enemy is man!

Farther along, the great torrent of water pouring into Reservoir 6 is ducted from another reservoir in an extensive system. Hartford gets most of its water from the Shepaug and Barkhamstead Reservoirs in northern Connecticut; the West Hartford Reservoirs serve largely for holding and storage rather than as prime sources of water.

Continue along the west shore of the reservoir. Cross the bridge at the end of the reservoir (1.7 miles from the start) and follow the blue-blazed woods road nearly ½ mile to the "TRAIL" sign at left. Follow this trail up to a low-use tar road about three miles from your start. Follow this road uphill (to your right) to the Heublein Tower, the fourth and most ornate tower situated on this ridge top. Built in 1914, this structure was home to the family of Gilbert Heublein, the liquor magnate, for over thirty years. On a clear day the sharp-eyed can survey 1,200 square miles from the top; on the northern horizon you can pick out New Hampshire's Mount Monadnock (the second most climbed mountain in the world—the first is Mount Fuji in Japan) some eighty miles to the north; the Berkshires in western Massachusetts; the hills of eastern Rhode Island; and Long Island Sound to the south.

After enjoying the view, proceed south along the cliff escarpment past a huge roofed-over barbecue pit, through a picnic area, and past a pavilion which has a lovely view across the Farmington River Valley. A couple of side paths to the right lead to cliff views somewhat limited by vegetation.

Continue on the escarpment path until you come to large yellow "No Trespassing" signs. At this point bushwhack

Looking west from the escarpment

directly away from the cliff (east) about 100 yards to the tar road you came up on earlier. Proceed downhill and turn left at the first fork on the trail you came up on. In ½ mile cross the power line. Continuing on this route past a tote road entering at left, you reach a hard-packed dirt road in another ¼ mile—the blue-blazed Metacomet Trail. Turn right.

After the trail passes the pipeline clearing there is a fork at the head of the reservoir. Bear left to survey the east shore. As you top a hill, the Metropolitan District Commission's filtration plant for Bloomfield comes into view. Beyond it is the ever-growing Hartford skyline. The dirt road joins and briefly follows the plant's tar road along the wooded shore.

Keep along the reservoir, following the lesser used tar road. This road turns to dirt in a few yards and follows the length of the reservoir bank. As you look back, the Heublein Tower thrusts above the ridge. The rock riprap lining the banks below you retards erosion.

When you come to a tar road again, stay on the path between it and the water. At the fork, bear left uphill away from the reservoir (a right turn will take you out to the end of a point of land that is worth the detour). After crossing a causeway, you soon emerge on the road within sight of the parking lot.

38

People's Forest

Total Distance: 7 miles
Time: 4 hours
Rating: C
Highlights: Views, secluded woods
Maps: USGS 7½' Winsted, New Hartford

Good hiking trails do not just happen nor are they maintained effortlessly. Three groups maintain most of Connecticut's trails. The Connecticut Chapter of the Appalachian Mountain Club does an excellent job of covering the Appalachian Trail. The unpaid volunteers of the Connecticut Forest and Park Association maintain the extensive Blue Trail system. Because each trail section in this system is the domain of a single individual who is subject to the vagaries of time and temperament, occasionally a section of blue-blazed trail is slightly unkempt. But overall, these volunteers do a superb job as well. The trails maintained by the State are by far the most poorly kept. While some parks and forests have enough tax money and personnel to keep their trails in tiptop shape, the People's State Forest is an example of an excellent trail system that lately (1983) has suffered from lack of both (this can change from year to year, so when you go this area may be well-maintained while another may have deteriorated). In the fall of 1990, these trails were freshly blazed, so don't miss this hike—it is a good one—but save it until you are sure of yourself in the woods. These

trails need some clearing but with a bit of care you should not have trouble following them.

From the junction of CT 318 and US 44 east of Winsted proceed east on CT 318 across the Farmington River and take the first left (East River Road). In .8 mile, by the People's Forest sign, fork right on the gated, paved state forest road. (You have missed your turn if you come to a picnic area.) Then, in .2 mile, turn left up a short gravel road to a parking lot by a well-built but now vacant trailside museum.

A trail, blazed orange on blue, starts into the woods here on your right. Follow this path. Shortly the blue-blazed Robert Ross Trail breaks off to the left; stay on the orange-on-blue-blazed Agnes Bowen Trail as it curves through a white pine grove to a tar road. Follow the road downhill (right) a few yards, then go left into the woods by a forest "Trail" sign. Almost immediately you cross a small stream, which the now rocky trail follows uphill to the left. In .56 mile the trail passes through a roadside picnic area, bears right by a fireplace, and in another .67 mile intersects the Charles Pack Trail (yellow on blue).

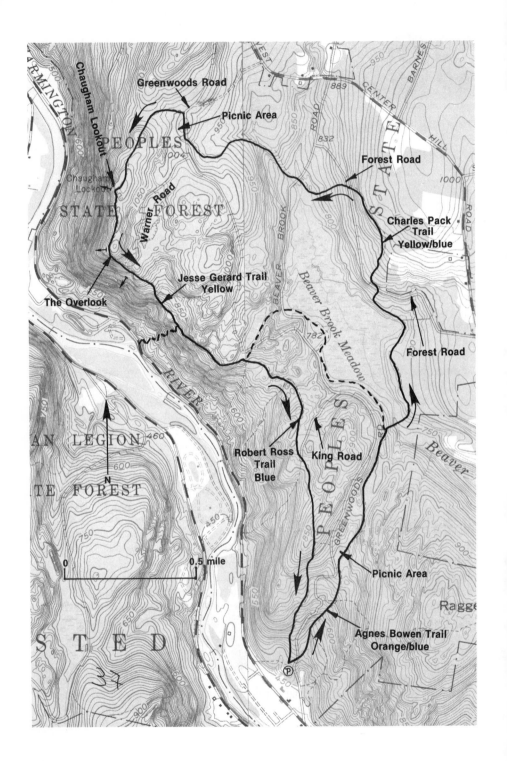

Greenwoods Road

Picnic Area

Chaugham Lookout

PEOPLES

Chaugham Lockout

STATE FOREST

Warner Road

The Overlook

Jesse Gerard Trail
Yellow

Forest Road

Charles Pack
Trail
Yellow/blue

Forest Road

Beaver Brook Meadow

BEAVER BROOK

AN LEGION

N

TE FOREST

Robert Ross
Trail
Blue

King Road

GREENWOODS RD

Picnic Area

Ragge

Agnes Bowen Trail
Orange/blue

Beaver

STED

0   0.5 mile

P

Turn right to follow these blazes. In a few yards you reach Beaver Brook which you cross on a footbridge built by the Youth Conservation Corps in 1976. On the right you can see the old high-water double cable crossing; the cable crossing was used by walking on the lower cable and holding onto the upper one for balance.

After crossing the footbridge, bear left across the hill side, keeping the beaver pond of Beaver Brook on your left, and then curve right uphill. In .71 mile from the junction with the orange-on-blue-blazed trail, you cross gravel Pack Grove Road. You cross it again in another .48 mile and then drop downhill for .21 mile to recross the brook on Beaver Brook Road bridge. Watch for trout swimming in the crystal water under the bridge. The trail reenters the woods on the stream's far side and shortly fords a small feeder brook. Another .58 mile of woods walking brings you to Greenwoods Road where this trail ends.

Step across the pavement and cut to the right through the picnic area to another "Trail" sign on your left. Here you pick up the Jesse Gerard Trail which leads you back toward your car. Note the poisonous metallic-blue clintonia berries beside the path here. Although occasionally found locally, this wide-leaved lily is more common in northern New England.

This trail, blazed in yellow, traces an old tote road for a short distance before taking an obscure path uphill. After passing between two huge glacial boulders .32 miles from Greenwoods Road, the trail turns right toward Chaugham Lookout. These open ledges .47 mile from Greenwoods Road provide an excellent view northwest across a wide, wild, wooded valley. The canoe-dotted Farmington River winds sinuously below. The well-worn trail continues through hemlocks along the ledge escarpment, reaching the overlook in .30 mile.

Proceeding steeply down, you find sweet lowbush blueberries flanking the trail over erosion-bared traprock. The yellow-blazed Jesse Gerard and blue-blazed Robert Ross trails run together here. They split about three-quarters of a mile from Chaugham Lookout. (The yellow blazed trail turns right and descends 299 steps to an old Indian settlement called Barkhamsted Lighthouse.) Continuing on the blue-blazed trail another .88 mile, you hit the terminus of gravel King Road. Turn right down the tote road that is marked at the start by a fence post with an orange blaze. Be careful here—the blue-blazed trail makes an obscure left turn in less than 100 yards where the tote road curves right. Stay with the blue blazes.

Continue downhill on the blue trail to the orange-on-blue trail near the deserted museum. Follow the blazes to the right back to your car.

Macedonia Brook

Total Distance: 6.7 miles
Time: 4 hours
Rating: B
Highlight: Views
Maps: USGS 7½' Ellsworth, Amenia NY-Ct.

A cluster of hills 1,000 to 1,400 feet high, separated by pure clear Macedonia Brook, makes up Macedonia Brook State Park. This 2,294 acre park contains 13 miles of trail. The famed Appalachian Trail used to run through Macedonia Brook, but it was relocated in the late 1980s—now what was the AT is part of the Connecticut Blue Trail system.

Macedonia Brook lies just inside Connecticut's western boundary. From the junction of CT 341 and US 7 in Kent, take CT 341 west for 1.7 miles to Macedonia Brook Road, where a sign directs you into the park down a paved road on the right. The loop hike described here is the Macedonia Ridge Trail and starts at the trailhead about .75 mile from the park entrance.

Cross the bridge over the brook and shortly enter the woods at left. Slab the hillside and at the junction with the red trail, turn sharply left and climb the ridge. The remnants of an old apple orchard bisect the trail; many of the gnarled unkept specimens still bloom each spring.

After another half mile, the Yellow Trail branches to the left as our trail bends

right. In another .5 mile, the Green Trail comes in at left from the park road. The Blue and Green Trails run together right on the old tote road. Shortly our Blue Trail turns left off the road (the Green Trail continues down the road and out to Fuller Mountain Road). Stay on the Blue Trail.

A short distance beyond the Green Trail you walk past several clumps of grey birches on the left. These dowdy cousins of the sparkling white birch have a greyer bark that is not inclined to peel with age. A short-lived tree with triangular leaves and black triangular patches beneath the base of each limb, the gray birch is an early colonizer of uncultivated open fields.

Our trail climbs easily and steadily up and over a col between two unnamed peaks. In spring the greenish-yellow flowers of the many short-lived striped maples here lend a faint but delightful fragrance to the woods. The flower clusters dangle from the branches like exotic earrings.

From the col, the Blue Trail drops steeply down to a deeply worn old town road (the former AT) one mile from the Green Trail. At the barricade, our trail

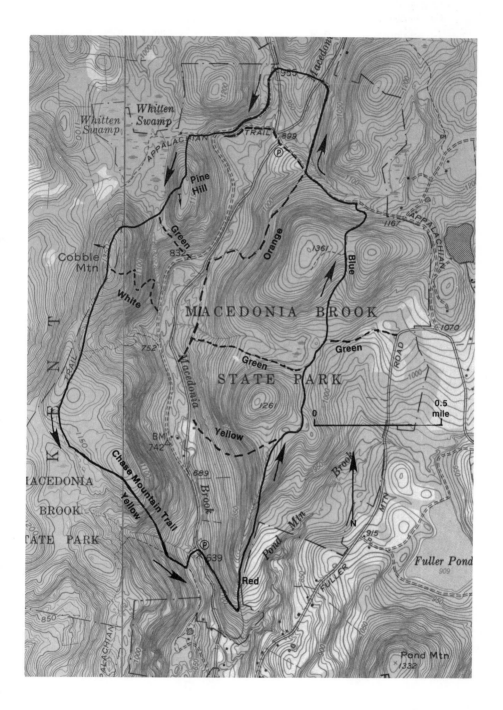

turns right and crosses a brook. In just under .5 mile turn left on dirt Keeler Road. Cross bridge and turn right. Follow the brook, then climb to good views in .5 mile. Switch back down, turn left on Weber Road, then turn right on the old CCC road before turning left uphill to begin the ascent of Pine Hill. Beneath an ash tree on the right we found two morels. Acclaimed as our best tasting local wild mushroom, this hollow, light brown fungus with its exterior raised latticework is the elusive treasure of the dedicated mycologist.

At the top of the grade, the trail turns left into the woods climbing steadily and fairly steeply. In June a few pink azaleas or June pinks spot the trail with color and fragrance. Threading through the laurel undergrowth, the grade eases as you near the top of Pine Hill. (As on most Connecticut hills, the steepest slope on Pine Hill is in the middle of the grade.)

From the ledges on Pine Hill's far side, you have an excellent view down the valley. Close by from right to left are Cobble Mountain, South Cobble Mountain (both of which you climb on this hike), and Chase Mountain. In the center distance are Mounts Algo and Schaghticoke.

Follow the trail down over steep ledges, passing a green-blazed trail, left, in the col. Continuing uphill, the trail steepens considerably and then eases again as it passes several large beds of wild oats with their drooping bell-shaped flowers.

Be prepared for superb views when you reach the top of Cobble Mountain (.9 mile from Pine Hill), for the trail traverses its exposed western escarpment. The ridge across the valley is in New York and beyond it are the Catskills. By dropping down the ledges a bit you get a good view of Connecticut's northwest corner—the Riga Plateau. The tallest peak (topped by a fire tower) on the far right is Mount Everett in Massachusetts. To its left is Bear Mountain in Connecticut (see Hike 40).

Continue on these exposed ledges to their far end where Cobble Mountain Trail (white blazes) comes in from the left. Stay on the blue trail which drops steeply down the ledges into the col before rising gradually up South Cobble Mountain. The trail passes to the left of the summit. Then follow the steep rocky route down into the col. Head downhill for .6 mile to the park road. Follow the pavement right to the parking lot and your car.

Bear Mountain Loop

Total Distance: 6.5 miles
Time: 5 hours
Rating: AB
Highlights: Connecticut's highest summit, rock scrambling,
  views
Map: USGS 7½' Bashbish Falls

A rugged, windswept mountain with views into three states awaits you at the high point of this hike. On the way, you hike a portion of the justly famous Appalachian Trail (AT). At the top of Bear Mountain there is a once magnificent stone monument (see picture of what existed in 1977) that has partially crumbled but is still an imposing mass. In late 1983 the rubble was stabilized, creating a lower monument. This monument was erected to proclaim (incorrectly) this as the highest point in Connecticut. In fact, as has been discovered since World War II, the state's high point is on a shoulder of Mount Frissel, whose summit is in Massachusetts.

To reach the start of this hike, drive on CT 41 3.2 miles north from its junction with US 44 in Salisbury. There is a small hikers' parking lot on the left. (*Caution*—during early spring the mud here may be a problem.)

The blue-blazed Undermountain Trail—a feeder to the AT—starts at the parking lot and soon passes a large bulletin board which carries the latest trail information. There is a container with a constantly replenished supply of AT information folders attached to the board. The folders contain handy parking, camping, and route information.

Proceed across a flat field that is rapidly becoming overgrown. We have watched this area change from an open field to virtual woodlands in just ten years! Enter the woods where the trail starts to climb, gently at first, and then more steeply. This trail presents an almost unrelieved climb to its junction with the AT in 1.9 miles. It is a good test of wind and muscle and an excellent place to practice the mile-eating trick used by seasoned hikers: set a pace you can maintain all the way to the top without stopping.

After .25 mile, you pass an eroded gully on the right and the hulks of several large fallen chestnut trees on the left. Although these trees have been dead for at least seventy years, their dissolving trunks still litter the forest floor. The barkless remains, slowly decomposing, have a weatherbeaten look unlike any other dead tree. Chestnut trees rot from the inside out, thereby maintaining their size and apparent integrity longer than most dead trees.

As you climb, it becomes more obvious that this trail is an old tote road whose surface has eroded several feet into the hill. This erosion was probably caused by countless horsehauled loads scoring the surface, with rain and snowmelt doing the rest. Soon you encounter a bad washout. This unsightly scar was at least partially caused by hikers! The constant tramping of feet killed the stabilizing vegetation, and the deeply eroded road did not permit the diversion of running water off the trail. Then a real gully-washer of a storm, probably in the spring when the soil was already saturated and unstable, overnight caused the muddy earth to slide into the ravine at left, leaving the gouge on the trail you see before you. Since the water now flows into the ravine instead of down the trail, and the Appalachian Mountain Club has rerouted the trail off the worst

areas, the rest of the road should be fairly secure.

A couple tenths of a mile above the washout go right off of the Undermountain Trail onto blue-blazed Paradise Lane (nicely signed). Blazed trails may use many different colors, but the white blazes are reserved for the AT. This blue-blazed trail joins the AT north of the summit of Bear Mountain in 2.1 miles. If you had continued straight on the Undermountain Trail you would meet the AT south of the peak of Bear Mountain (you will come back this way on this described circuit).

Paradise Lane starts roughly parallel to the AT. In a short distance, the trail goes left off the old tote road and zigzags steeply up the hill. At a relatively flat area on Bear Mountain the trail levels a bit and even eases gently downhill until it reaches a swampy area on the side of this mountain.

Along this section of the trail Gerry had a special experience. A ruffed grouse took off with the usual thunder of wings without having run a ways as they usually do. Why did she hold in one spot so long before flying? Having visually noted where she took off, Gerry went over and found a rough circular nest with nine buff eggs in it.

After going along the level a ways you will see the very steep south side of Bear Mountain at left. Cross a small seasonal stream and continue curving gently left. Soon you reach a small "pond" (the water is mostly filled with bushes). After crossing the pond's outlet stream, note the northeast corner of Bear Mountain as you go across an open ledge decorated with laurel and huckleberry. The line between Connecticut and Massachusetts is marked with yellow paint.

The monument in 1977

The "new" monument on Bear Mountain

You reach the AT in a hemlock area, then turn left (south). A right turn will take you to Katahdin in about 800 miles. For years, members of the Appalachian Mountain Club used a group of five short-lived white birches to know where to turn off onto this end of Paradise Lane from the AT. Now that the National Park Service has bought this land, it is rather appropriate that as of June 1983 two of these birches had fallen.

Go diagonally left up the rocky AT on Bear Mountain. Some professional trail crew work has been done here in stabilizing this steep route with large erosion-proof rocks. After a long stretch the trail turns directly up the steep, ledge-dominated slope. After several steep pitches, where you have to use both hands and feet, the AT enters some stunted scrub pine that perches precariously on rather bare open ledges. Almost immediately you will spot the monument remains on top of Bear Mountain.

While strolling around the open top, watch for large, dark, soaring birds—turkey vultures. These birds, with a six foot wing-span, are the largest of North America's vultures. They are common in the adjacent Hudson River Valley and are spreading through the northeast. They use rising columns of air along the edge of the Riga Plateau to soar for hours without flapping their wings.

From the summit, the views are superb. To the east lie the Twin Lakes and Canaan Mountain. For the best view to the north, follow the AT north to a ledge on the edge of the stand of scrub pines. The mountain with a tower is Mount Everett (2,602 feet), the apex of the second highest mountain mass in Massachusetts. The hulk in front of Everett is Race Mountain (2,365 feet).

When you are ready, follow the AT off the top. Just as the trail starts seriously downward there is a grand view to the south and west. Ahead is the relatively level Riga Plateau. To the right the mountains that you see are, from left to right, Gridley (CT), North and South Brace (NY), Round Mountain (CT) with Mount Frissell (MA) behind it, and north of Frissell (you will have to go down the path a bit to see this past obstructing trees) is Ashley (MA). The body of water left of Gridley is South Pond (1,715 feet), and the Catskills can be seen off in the distance on a clear day. It usually takes several visits before these mountains become old friends, but the journeys are definitely worth the effort! As we sit at home, we can picture this area in our mind's eye. When you can do that their beauty is yours forever.

Continue, passing several scrub pines whose wind-distorted shapes would do credit to a bonsai artist. All lean east, away from the prevailing west winds. With infinite patience, the cold, desiccating winds have carved off any upward shoots that braved the elements so that the tops are flattened and stream eastward—the path of least resistance.

As you progress downwards, the various hardy oaks rise slowly to obscure your view. Then you rise into the open again to a partial view of the mountains. However, each dip carries you into higher and higher trees until the trees win this game of hide-and-seek.

About .6 mile from the summit, a tote road comes in on your right from gravel Mount Washington Road—bear left on the AT. In another .2 mile, the blue-blazed Undermountain Trail leaves left steeply downhill. Take this trail; it leads you to your car in 1.9 miles.

Windsor Locks Canal

Total Distance: 9 miles
Time: 4½ hours
Rating: D
Highlights: Historic canal, riverside vegetation, wildlife
Maps: USGS 7½' Windsor Locks, Broad Brook

By the mid-nineteenth century stiff competition from railroads had combined with a shortage of bulk materials and an uncompromising terrain to bring about the collapse of New England's expanding canal system. The Windsor Locks Canal, built in 1829 to bypass the Enfield Rapids on the Connecticut River, was an exception. Here the canal survived because water diverted from New England's biggest river not only served barge traffic but also provided power to several mills, the last of which continued to operate until the 1930s. Today the Windsor Locks Canal still routes an occasional pleasure craft around the rapids, and its old towpath, now paved, offers a pleasant level trail for walking or bicycling.

To reach the towpath, follow CT 159 south from its southern junction with CT 190 for .1 mile to Canal Road on the left. The road ends in about .4 mile with a large parking lot on your left. The size of the lot is not indicative of trail use; it is heavily used by fishermen who congregate here from April to June. The famous Enfield Rapids provide the best ocean-run shad fishing in New England.

Head south down the river; pass through the gates and over the canal to the start of the towpath. The impressive Enfield Rapids dominate the scene to your left. Your route simply follows the paved way 4.5 miles to its end; there are no side trails to mislead you. The towpath is a designated bicycle trail, so please give cyclists the right of way.

While the plants and wildlife along the way are the chief attractions of this hike, man-made constructions along the canal are not without interest. About two miles from the start, the blunt prow of heavily wooded, mile-long King's Island comes into view. Notice here that the banks of the canal are made of the soft Connecticut Valley red sandstone (perhaps this material is best known as the rock used to build New York City's brownstone apartments). About a third of a mile along King's Island, you cross a small overflow dam built to handle the flood waters of Strong Brook; smaller streams run directly into the canal. A quarter mile below King's Island, you will pass alongside venerable stone abutments supporting a trestle over the Connecticut River; several trains whistled by as we hiked the towpath.

As you walk, maintain an alert eye.

This entire trip is a veritable oasis in an urban desert. While man creates monotonous conformity, nature in her toughness moves in wherever possible.

We came upon a young woodchuck caught between the devil (us) and the deep blue sea (the canal). Butterflies were constant companions. Besides the cabbage white (the only butterfly that is a common agricultural pest), we saw various swallowtails, skippers, wood satyrs, and a beloved ally, the red admiral, whose caterpillar ravages nettles.

From a botanical point of view, this walk is one of the best in the state. We identified ox-eye daisies, fleabane, yarrow, vetch, two varieties of milkweed, campion, St. Johnswort, black-eyed Susans, several goldenrods, mullein, deadly nightshade, thimbleweed, Deptford pinks, plaintains (American and English), both bull and Canada thistle, roses, gill-over-the-ground, jewelweed, day lilies, and lovely sundrop—like giant buttercups with cross-shaped stigmas. The clovers, legumes with built-in nitrogen factories on their roots, are well represented. In addition to white and alsike clover, we found at least two varieties of yellow-blossomed hop clovers.

Vines and bushes abound; poison ivy, several varieties of grapes, Virginia creeper, Oriental bittersweet, sweet-smelling Japanese honeysuckle, scrub willow, various types of the smaller dogwoods, elderberries, alder (both smooth and speckled), sassafras, juniper, slippery elm, and smooth and staghorn sumacs with their great masses of red-ripening acid fruit.

Here also treetops that you usually see only from below stand open for your scrutiny. These trees growing along the riverbed, or on the steep canal sides to your left, present their seldom-seen tops for your curiosity. The

round buttons that give the sycamore one of its common names (buttonwood) are here at eye level, and the stickiness of the butternut tree's immature nuts can be tested in place. In mid to late May the fluffs of cotton from the aptly named eastern cottonwood fill the air—in places we have seen a gossamer layer of this cotton two inches deep on the ground. In early summer you can pick with ease the tasty fruit of the red mulberry—if you can beat the birds!

We talk of waste areas, but probably the only true wastelands are those areas sealed with concrete and asphalt—and even these are transitory. A constant rain of seeds awaits the smallest moistened crack, ready to sprout and grow. Near the end of the towpath, we found that a clump of field bindweed had wrestled a foothold in the junction between an old brick building and the asphalt drive. In the wild the small white morning glory-like flowers of this "weed" have little appeal for most of us, but here they lighten a dingy corner.

A second set of gates 4.5 miles from the first marks the end of the towpath near CT 140. Turn around and retrace your steps to your car.

A young woodchuck along the towpath

Seven Falls

Total Distance: 7.5 miles
Time: 4½ hours
Rating: C
Highlights: Views, well laid-out trail
Map: USGS 7½' Middle Haddam

Laying out a hiking trail is more of an art than a science; the shortest distance between two points does not necessarily provide the most interesting hiking. A trail that is properly laid out directs you to the best of an area's natural features, thus offering you the finest hike possible. This stretch of the Mattabesett Trail, which starts at Seven Falls south of Middletown, does just that. Its corkscrew route approaches, circles, and often climbs the boulders and rock ridges that are so characteristic of the local terrain.

Another attraction of this hike is the number of loop trails. The main trail is blazed with blue rectangles and the loop trails, generally shorter, are marked with blue circles. We suggest that you go out on the main trail and return on the blue circle loops to maximize hike variety. While our route follows the Mattabesett Trail as far as Bear Hill and returns on several loops for a distance of 7.5 miles, you can shorten the hike by taking only the first or the first two loops for a total distance of 2.5 or 5.5 miles respectively. This hike is far more difficult to describe than to follow, as the junctions are well signed to assist you in finding your way.

The hike begins by the Seven Falls Roadside Park on CT 154 south of Middletown. Leave CT 9 on exit 10 (Aircraft Road) and follow CT 154 south (right) for .8 mile. The park is on your left.

Leave your car and thread your way through the picnic area to the crystal clear brook tumbling over a series of small falls in the boulder-choked stream for which the park is named. Follow the brook a short distance upstream to the highway bridge, cross over, and enter the woods on the right. The rectangular blue blazes of the Mattabesett Trail lead back down the brook to the falls area. About 100 yards from the road, turn left at the double blaze (the upper blaze is displaced in the direction of the turn) by a smaller brook. As we followed this brook upstream in early spring, we watched a water snake wind its way along the brook bottom. Not once did we see him come up for air.

Picnickers have worn an aimless labyrinth of trails through this section; most go nowhere so be careful to stick with the blue blazes. Shortly you cross this smaller brook and wind up on a wooded hill. You soon reach and cross an old tote road; at a second tote road

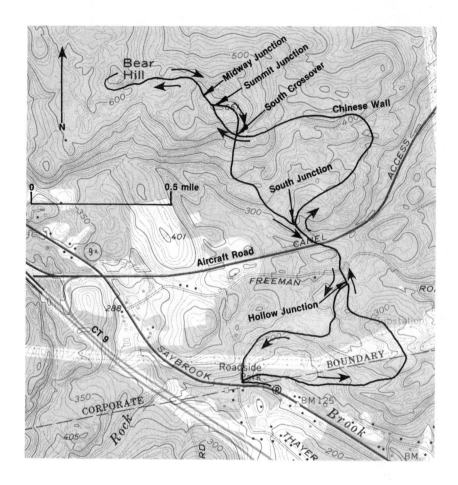

go left, paralleling the power line. Along this stretch the trail skirts, surmounts, and circles numerous ledges and boulders. In .6 mile you pass a Middletown/ Haddam boundary marker — a cross piece with "M/H" on it on a rod set into a rock. From several vantage points you can survey numerous forested, rolling hills with only a few houses nestled here and there.

Two high-voltage power lines cut through the woods .2 mile further on. Be careful of this and all such crossings. The route rarely goes straight across the clearing, and except for a possible blaze on the poles there are usually no markers between the parallel, but widely separated, forest walls. In partial compensation, the blazes on the forest edges are often deliberately made larger.

When you reach Hollow Junction, the first blue circle loop heads back the general way you came (about 1.4 miles from the start). This alternate trail, 1.2 miles long, leads you back to the falls area.

Continuing straight ahead on the main

Nature's tic-tac-toe

trail, you cross tarred Freeman Road in about .1 mile, and then in another .1 mile, tarred Aircraft Road (labelled Canal Access on the map). Climb the hill to South Junction (1.7 miles from the start), where a second loop trail breaks off. Keep to the main trail, which forks to the right. The path tends generally uphill at first and then heads down, crossing a brook several times before climbing another ridge about one mile from South Junction. You cross another brook and scramble over ledges and atop the "Chinese Wall" before reaching South Crossover, 1.7 miles from South Junction. This circle loop winds about .5 mile back to South Junction.

Continuing on the main trail, you reach Summit Junction about .2 mile from South Crossover. In another .1 mile, you come to Midway Junction. Climb to the top of Bear Hill (640 feet) on the main trail (rectangles) in another .5 mile, about 4.2 miles from the start. Look for the two geological survey bench markers—one to the right, one to the left. The profusion of huckleberries here was a major attraction for bears, hence the probable origin for its name.

Retrace your steps from the top of Bear Hill to Summit Junction. Then, on your return, follow the blue circle trails beginning at Summit Junction whenever they are available to provide you with different territory. It is about 2.7 miles from Summit Junction to your car by the blue circle trails.

Mansfield Hollow

Total Distance: 8 miles
Time: 4½ hours
Rating: CD
Highlights: River walk, view
Map: USGS 7½' Spring Hill

Because of its proximity to the University of Connecticut at Storrs, the Mansfield Hollow Recreation Area is sprinkled with temporary refugees from academia: jogging professors, strolling students, and young families with toddlers. In addition to picnic tables, fireplaces, ball fields, bridle paths, rest rooms, and boat launching facilities, Mansfield Hollow also encompasses one of the two southern termini of the Nipmuck Trail, which stretches thirty-four miles north to Bigelow Hollow State Park near the Massachusetts border. This hike follows the blue-blazed Nipmuck Trail through a flood control area and rolling countryside as far as "50 Foot," a nice little lookout.

From the junction of CT 89 and CT 195 in Mansfield Center, drive south on CT 195 for .5 mile to Bassett Bridge Road and turn left. After .8 mile, park in the lot on the right side of the entrance road to Mansfield Hollow Dam Recreation Area.

To reach the start of the Nipmuck Trail, follow the gravel entrance road through the open fields to the pine-fringed woods, where the road along a flood control causeway on the left leads to a gated woods road. Turning right, you soon find the Nipmuck's blue blazes leading into the pine woods on the left. (You can see the flood control reservoir at the end of the woods road.)

The trail starts on sandy soil, where white pines grow very well. You reach a woods road in .1 mile; the blazes lead to the right before turning left into the woods—again the reservoir is visible at the end of the road. On your right are patches of shinleaf, which you can distinguish by their almost round evergreen leaves. Although you will not see their spikes of nodding white flowers until June or July, the flower buds may be found nestled beneath forest detritus in early May. This plant derives its name from the early custom of applying its leaves to sores and bruises—any plaster, no matter where applied, was called a shin plaster.

As you wend your way up onto a flat, the trail touches and then heads left off a bridle path. You will flirt with numerous bridle paths strewn with strawberry plants and cinquefoils through the first part of the hike. The mixture gives you a chance to distinguish between these two plants with similar leaves: the

strawberry has three-leaved bunches, the local cinquefoils, five.

Beneath a blue-blazed white pine you will find the first of many hawthorns along the trail. This shrub is characterized by formidable two-inch thorns, attractive white flowers with a rather disagreeable odor, and fall pomes suitable for making jelly. You encounter and cross a second bridle path, pass through a third wooded section, and emerge once again on a bridle path.

At this junction, head right. After curving left through a small patch of woods, the trail continues along the right side of a ball field on a gravel road to CT 89, 1.5 miles from the start. Follow paved CT 89 left briefly and then cross to a grassy area. Bear right into the woods, then continue downhill by an old well and cellar hole. Cross the abandoned tar road. Soon the trail goes left on a dirt road to the bottom of a dry dike. In flood times the central gates of the flood control dam can be closed to limit downstream water flow. Several such dikes are found in this flood control area. Cross the small streams below the dike on two footbridges.

At the far end of the dike turn right into the woods. White oak (the bark is actually light grey) stands sentinel on the trail. When you reach a gravel road, turn left.

A utility pole footbridge carries the trail across the Fenton River. Blue blazes and painted wooden arrows guide you through this stretch. Robins run ahead of you in the grass, and the soulful cry of the mourning dove echoes around you.

The path now angles up onto a small gravel ridge deposited by the glacier with the river below at left. To the left a small stream widens into swamp pools liberally populated with frogs and painted turtles. Dropping off the ridge, you continue through a meadow brilliant with the bright yellows of the goldfinch and the swallowtail butterfly. Turn left into the woods just before you reach a second gravel ridge.

Shortly you come to the Fenton River again, which is spanned by another footbridge. After crossing, follow this thirty-foot wide trout river upstream (right) keeping a cornfield on your left. The trail winds among numerous fisherman's paths along the riverbank—watch the blazes carefully to avoid straying. Ferns grace the low spots, while the aptly named interrupted fern stands tall throughout.

Two miles from CT 89 the trail cuts to the left away from the river and uphill to Chaffeeville Road. The trail crosses the road and rolls through hardwoods and hemlocks. About 25 yards beyond the second stream crossing, you reach the junction with the southern section of the Nipmuck Trail which starts at Puddin' Lane in Mansfield. Go right (north) and hike along the base of a large outcropping. Columbine hangs from the dripping-wet rock cliffs on the left.

Beyond the drier cliffs higher up, just before the blue-blazed trail bears right steeply downhill, leave the Nipmuck Trail and follow an unmarked trail left up along the base of the cliff. Known locally as "50 Foot," this lookout offers fine views of the Eastern Connecticut woodlands.

Enjoy your lunch with a view and then retrace your steps to your car.

On the Nipmuck Trail

Cockaponset

Total Distance: 10.1 miles
Time: 5½ hours
Rating: CD
Highlights: Reservoirs, well laid-out trail, woodland brooks
Map: USGS 7½' Haddam

Cockaponset State Forest is a 15,000 acre monument to the Civilian Conservation Corps (CCC). In its heyday (1933-1941), this state forest had three encampments with a force three times that now employed for the entire state forest system. The passage of fifty-five years has not obliterated the roadside fireholes, stonework ditches, stepped trails, and tasteful plantings.

This hike starts by Pattaconk Reservoir in Chester. From CT 9 take exit 6 to CT 148. Follow this road west for 1.5 miles to Cedar Lake Road and turn right. Go 1.5 miles to entrance to Lake Pattaconk Recreation Area and turn left. In .4 mile (past the beach), there is a parking lot on both the left and the right sides of the road.

You are at the Filley Road crossing of the Cockaponset Trail. This 10.1 mile hike does three consecutive loops and may easily be shortened to 2.3 or 5.8 miles by taking just the first or the first two loops. The entire trail has been wheeled (the distances have been accurately measured using a calibrated wheel), and at all junctions away from the road crossings there are signs posting distances to various spots on the

trail. Signs are notoriously hard to maintain at road crossings as they are too tempting a target for vandals and souvenir hunters. Our hike follows the Cockaponset Trail (blue blazes) north to Beaver Brook junction and returns using the loop trails (red dot on a blue blaze) wherever possible.

Proceed through the parking lot on the east (right) side of the road, following the blue blazes as the trail leaves the left end of the parking lot. Our trail soon goes right on a gravel road to Pattaconk crossing #4—stay on the blue-blazed Cockaponset Trail heading north to old County Road. Cross a series of three woodland brooks, each one more lovely than the one before; all three flow into Pattaconk Reservoir.

In 1977, when we first scouted this trail, literally thousands of chipmunks enlivened these woods. In 1983 we didn't see any. Chipmunks, like many of the small mammals whose numbers are not effectively limited by predators, go through population cycles. From a very low point, their numbers increase steadily year by year until they seem to be everywhere; then disease and/or starvation decimates their population and the cycle starts over again.

After crossing several more streams, the trail climbs and then descends gently to Pattaconk Brook at junction #5, 1.2 miles from the car. This is the most difficult stream crossing of this hike. In 1983, Sue fell in on the way out and elected to just wade through it on her return. This is where you return on the Pattaconk Trail if you wish to do only the 2.3 mile option.

Stay on the blue blazes, reaching another brook crossing in .3 mile at North Pattaconk junction #6. Just before the junction look for the patch of cardinal flowers. Here we rejoin the original Cockaponset Trail, which is well-worn and easy to follow. Continue for .8 mile to unpaved Old County Road. In spring the ledges in this section are decorated with dwarf ginseng, white violets, wood anemone, Solomon's-seal, and a profusion of mountain laurel.

Proceed left on County Road for about .1 mile before turning right on a tote road. On your left is a laurel covered hillside, on your right a brushy swamp. Follow the blue blazes north and uphill off the tote road, soon passing a small rock outcropping to overlook a dammed-up cattail swamp. Proceed with the swamp pond on your left, soon crossing the old dam. Originally built by the CCC in 1936, its height was increased three feet in 1979.

Our blue trail bears left along the pond through azaleas and laurel. Passing a boundary marker at the right (an iron pipe set in a pile of stones) and a rock jumble also at right, proceed through a lovely laurel tunnel to another large rock jumble at right. Soon the trail crosses a dirt road and reaches Jericho junction #9, 3.1 miles from the start. Here is where you can head back—following the red-dot-on-blue-blaze trail (Old Forest Trail)—if you wish to hike 5.8 miles.

Just before you reach graveled Jericho Road you pass a small stand of red spruce; this is the only native spruce found in any numbers in Connecticut. Its needle-covered twigs, when boiled with molasses or a similar sweetener and fermented, yield spruce beer, a good scurvy remedy.

Bear right a short distance on Jericho Road past an old CCC waterhole on your left, and then turn left back into the woods. Almost immediately you reach Wildwood junction #11—go right.

The next mile of trail to the second crossing of Jericho Road is a work of art; trail layout and construction at its

Small dam—Cockaponset State Forest

best. It is stepped, curbed, graded, and routed by all points of interest. It was constructed only incidently for the ease and comfort of the hiker; after forty years of use, trail erosion here is practically non-existent. Around Memorial Day weekend there are lady-slippers in bloom everywhere along this section for your enjoyment.

The trail in the midst of this scenic mile climbs and follows a brush-crowned rock ridge. Along this ridge are four spaced concrete blocks, the underpinnings of an old fire tower. These remnants tell two stories: the prominence of this ridge as a lookout and the substitution of modern, efficient fire-spotting planes. To reach a firetower with a warden standing his lonely vigil was a favorite goal for hikers—both for good views and good stories.

After crossing Jericho Road again, the laurel-lined trail passes several low, protruding ledges patched with large clumps of rock tripe. Shortly the trail skirts a swamp on the left which is sprinkled with tiny yellow spicebush blossoms in early spring.

About .5 mile from the road crossing watch the blue blazes carefully, as there are several unmarked trails leading left to the campground. Soon pass a small pond at right and go through the campground to cross Jericho Road again. Continue gently downhill then uphill through laurel. You first hear, then see the brook rushing along to your left. Cross the brook and continue through a small stand of hemlock to a huge downed hemlock at right—this giant broke off about 15 feet above the ground! Immediately cross another

brook before coming to Beaver Brook junction #14, 5.6 miles from the start.

Here we start our return. We will take the loop trail whenever possible, marked with a red dot on blue blazes. Leave the familiar blue blazes and bear left on Wildwood Trail. We meet and then cross a dirt road as the trail bends east and climbs to a wooded hilltop. Dropping down, the trail levels and continues through a laurel tunnel and then through pines.

Cross Jericho Road for the fourth and last time about 1.5 miles from junction #14. Now go left on Old Forest Trail, a deeply rutted tote road. Go left again on reaching Old County Road (gravel) and turn right into the woods after about .1 mile. When you come to the North Pattaconk junction #6 bear left on the Pattaconk Trail (this is a well-worn path, part of the old Cockaponset Trail). Shortly you reach a junction with a white trail—this is a horse trail that leads left around the reservoir. Stay on the red-dot-on-blue blazed foot trail.

Soon after crossing the brook at junction #5, the Pattaconk Reservoir starts to peek through the trees at left. In June 1990, the reservoir was nearly full and crowded with people on a hot Saturday afternoon. The rattling cry of the kingfisher frequently shatters the woodland silence here. From a well-sited perch these brilliant blue and white birds sight a small fish and make a head-first plunge into the water to snare it.

About 1 mile from junction #5 you reach Pattaconk Crossover #4. Here take the blue-blazed trail left to your parking lot.

Tunxis Ramble

Total Distance: 9.5 miles
Time: 5½ hours
Rating: C
Highlight: Mile of ledges.
Maps: USGS 7½' Thomaston, Bristol, Torrington, Collinsville

After a hiker gets his "sea legs," short, flat, often comparatively monotonous trails no longer have the appeal they once did. Aesthetic sense demands a more varied terrain; toughened muscles, more of a challenge. The lengthy Tunxis Ramble with its Mile of Ledges should satisfy both these needs nicely. The loop route described here makes a delightful hike through the forest north of Bristol, particularly in June when the laurel is in flower.

From the junction of CT 4 and CT 72 west of Burlington, proceed south of CT 72 for 4.4 miles. Turn left on East Church Road and after .7 mile park on the right opposite a gate. The Tunxis Trail, here marked with solid blue blazes, turns left off the road through the gateway. Blue blazes with a yellow dot in the center and blue blazes with a white dot in the center mark the routes on which you will complete this circuit.

Proceed along the well-beaten tote road. A little flower whose name rivals its delicate purple beauty, gill-over-the-ground is plentiful here. On the left at the edge of a large planting of red pine, a huge gnarled maple exudes character. The maple's twisting, wide-spreading

limbs grown over with green plants and fungi are only part of the attraction. Here is the commonplace, blown up to heroic proportions!

At the junction, bear left on the tote road as it passes a swamp filled with skunk cabbage. About .6 mile from the start, turn right as the blue-blazed trail heads to the "Mile of Ledges." (The yellow dot route proceeds straight to the Tory Den.) This part of the trail is a never-ending series of boulders, ledges, and cleft rocks. In June, the faint perfume and showy flowers of mountain laurel growing from dark recesses in moss-cushioned rocks heighten the beauty of each twist and turn. The trail crosses an old mill dam, or what is left of it; remnants of cement still hold some of the angular rocks. As you leave the ledges, the chugs and jug-a-rums of the green and bull frogs echo through the humid air.

When you reach paved Greer Road, 2.2 miles from the start, turn left. After about .5 mile, just before the pavement ends, the blue trail goes left into the woods and immediately reaches a junction. Here you take the trail marked with a yellow dot on a blue blaze right up

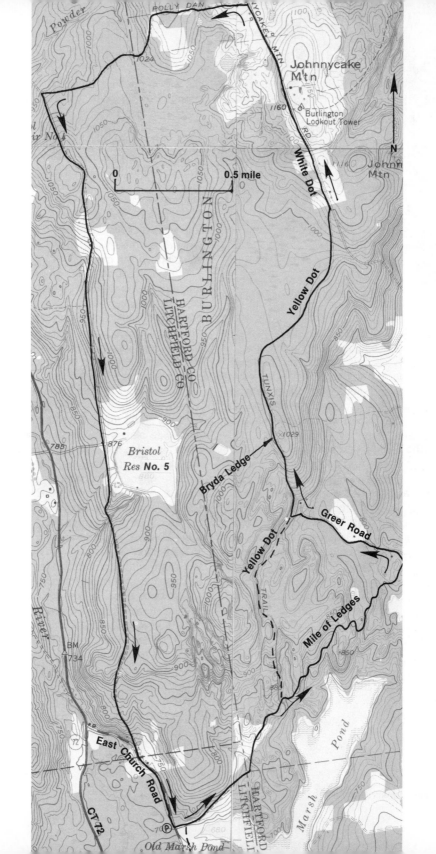

Along the Mile of Ledges

the hill. This passes near a house on the right. Please respect the right of the property owners; much of our hiking is done on private land and is a too easily lost privilege, not a right! Stout-stemmed bracken fern, a lover of dry ground, and yellow-blossomed whorled loosestrife are prevalent here.

The blue-on-yellow trail climbs over Bryda Ledge and soon reaches an old road. About one mile from the junction the trail bears left along the south slope of Johnnycake Mountain. After another .5 mile you reach gravel Johnnycake Mountain Road; follow the blazes, now blue with a centered white dot, to the left. The next mile of road walking takes you by a private game farm at the top of the hill. Strutting peacocks utter unearthly cries from their pens. (The peacocks' showy beauty is balanced by their loud—and anything but melodious—cry.) The sides of the road are rife with vegetation: meadow rue, angelica, wild geranium, yarrow, and horsemint are common, and an attractive alien that escaped from colonial gardens, the orange day lily, abounds.

After passing slightly west of Johnnycake Mountain, the trail turns left on tar Polly Dan Road. This road turns to dirt, deteriorates to two ruts in the grass, and finally becomes impassable to cars. You pass a pretty little pond filled with pollywogs on the right. Sweet fern and steeplebush are plentiful.

The tote road crosses a small stream; the large patch of trees on your left was killed when water from a beaver dam flooded its roots. Occasional toads and frogs jump through the grass. Short, dumpy hops identify the relatively enemyless toad; the wood frog makes long, energetic hops.

The tote road forks 1.1 mile from the Johnnycake Mountain Road (6.3 miles from the start); turn left with the blue and white blazes. You pass a house .5 mile down this lane—you are now on a very long private driveway. One mile further on, you cross Blueberry Hill Road and pass through a gate. Reservoir #5 is on the left. Continue straight on the gravel road on reservoir property. When the road bends left, proceed straight into the woods on an overgrown tote road with blue/white blazes. This trail continues downhill, crosses a brook, climbs once again, levels, then descends gradually, reaching a crushed rock driveway which leads to East Church Road. Your car is parked .4 mile down the road to the left.

Bolton Notch Railroad

Total Distance: 12 miles
Time: 6 hours
Rating: D
Highlights: Old railroad bed, notch
Map: USGS 7½' Rockville

Connecticut has many abandoned railroad beds cutting through interesting countryside. The victims of "progress," grasping management, and unreasonable unions, railroads—once the dominant method of moving freight—no longer exist in many parts of the country, and where they do, services are greatly reduced. This hike traverses a section of old roadbed where even the rails and ties have been removed.

Developers were poised to scoop up this land when a bill was passed in the State Legislature to make almost 20 miles of this abandoned railroad bed between Manchester and Willimantic a public scenic trail. So the land has been saved; it is up to us to adapt it for public use.

Because the old railroad beds were built to accommodate the great steam-breathing locomotives with their long strings of cars, hiking their routes is probably the fastest, easiest hiking one may find. The beds were flattened by cutting through hills and the resulting excess fill was used to build up depressions. When snow-covered, the roadbeds offer fine cross-country skiing.

To reach the start of this hike, follow

US 6 south from Bolton Notch for 3.5 miles past the Bolton/Coventry town line and go right. In about .2 mile, Bailey Road dead ends. There is ample room to park along the sides of the tar road. To begin this hike, just beyond the road go right on the flat, almost straight, gravel railroad bed.

For both the first and last three miles of this hike, you are always within earshot of US 6, and occasionally the road is visible through the trees. This section of railroad was discontinued in the 1960s and its rails and ties were removed during the 1970s.

While the undergrowth is inhibited by the dry, sterile gravel bed, young trees are slowly invading and narrowing the route. Occasional discarded wooden ties molder along the length of our hike; a couple of spare rails missed by the official scavengers can be seen resting on supports nearby. A cement water cistern is seen here and there.

Unfortunately a railroad bed accumulates man's debris. Most of the old refuse left by the railroad and telephone companies has decayed or been covered by nature. However, more recent droppings—cut brush and trees, old

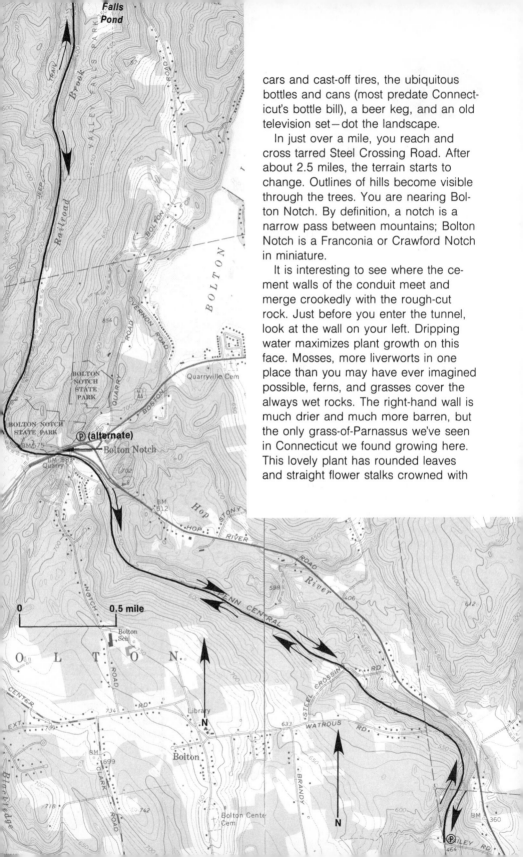

cars and cast-off tires, the ubiquitous bottles and cans (most predate Connecticut's bottle bill), a beer keg, and an old television set—dot the landscape.

In just over a mile, you reach and cross tarred Steel Crossing Road. After about 2.5 miles, the terrain starts to change. Outlines of hills become visible through the trees. You are nearing Bolton Notch. By definition, a notch is a narrow pass between mountains; Bolton Notch is a Franconia or Crawford Notch in miniature.

It is interesting to see where the cement walls of the conduit meet and merge crookedly with the rough-cut rock. Just before you enter the tunnel, look at the wall on your left. Dripping water maximizes plant growth on this face. Mosses, more liverworts in one place than you may have ever imagined possible, ferns, and grasses cover the always wet rocks. The right-hand wall is much drier and much more barren, but the only grass-of-Parnassus we've seen in Connecticut we found growing here. This lovely plant has rounded leaves and straight flower stalks crowned with creamy white blossoms whose petals are delicately etched with light green.

Bolton Notch is a good alternate starting point if you wish to break this hike in half. Instead of starting at Bailey Road, you may approach Bolton Notch from the east on US 44. Pass the small shopping center on the left and park well off the road just beyond Mac's Lunch on the right before the start of the guardrail.

Continue west, walking along the right side of the highway toward the notch. Stay off the road, as the traffic can be very heavy. Sassafras, slippery elm, grapevines, poison ivy, Virginia creeper,

Walking along the old grade

and dewberry grow along the roadside here. The late summer field bouquet includes Queen Anne's lace, yellow evening primrose, podded milkweed, burdock, black-eyed Susans, thistles, tick trefoil, boneset, ripening pokeberry, and jewelweed or touch-me-not, whose ripe flower pods will split beneath your touch and spit out seeds. During summer, while the woods are a uniform green, the meadows and fields are a riot of color.

Just past the large US Route 6 sign, follow a worn, unmarked path diagonally right down the steep bank. At the bottom of the gully turn left toward the railroad bed. Here and throughout this hike you may notice silvery angular rocks. If you look carefully at these rocks you may see little brownish-red nuggets. These are garnets, a semi-precious stone.

The cement conduit on your left is where you came in from Bailey Road. Go right down the railroad bed. The clearing at left was used by the railroad as a work area; wooden ties were creosoted here to lengthen their life.

The gravel railroad bed hugs the cut-rock walls which sometimes rise on both its sides. Nature can always yield new insights to the inquiring eye. Notice the trees taking root on the wall faces—a common sight on Connecticut walks. These trees are usually birch, occasionally maple, and almost never oak. Why? The weight of the seeds and their need for soil are major factors. Light seeds such as those of birch and maple lodge readily on the sides of the walls; moisture does the rest. Acorns, on the other hand, are heavy and need good deep soil, and so are rarely found on near steep wall faces. About .25 mile from the notch, a wooden bridge spans the

walls above you.

Often water that runs along the impervious ledges emerges at the rock cuts and runs down their side to the railroad bed below. This water feeds Railroad Brook at right, which will be your companion for the rest of the hike. A constant reminder of its presence is the sound of running water burbling over its rocky bottom.

Before too long the railroad bed is interrupted by a major washout—stay to the left. The stream that caused this washout (no doubt in flood) is now purring innocently under the bed. Neglected areas such as this are gradually reclaimed by nature.

Notice how the rock wall on the left has risen and steepened. The once level railroad bed is bumpy where trail bikes and all-terrain vehicles have passed through. You soon reach another washout; one section of the bed is covered with earth and debris. Discarded railroad ties and angular boulders carved from the rock cliffs are scattered along the way.

More than 2.5 miles from the notch, the cliffs at left get noticeably lower. Numerous grey birch line the bed. To your right you may glimpse the pond at Valley Falls Park, a recreational area owned and operated by the town of Vernon. Shortly, the railroad bed is crossed by a tote road; if followed to the right, this road reaches the shore of the pond. Our way curves left and soon parallels the tar road below. At this point turn around and retrace your steps to your car. The railroad bed continues east and south to the giant grain elevator in Manchester (reputed to be the largest in New England) where the tracks now end.

West Peak and Castle Crag

Total Distance: 8.2 miles
Time: 5½ hours
Rating: AB
Highlights: Excellent views, "Northern Island"
Map: USGS 7½' Meriden

Save this hike until your legs are in good shape (it's difficult), your mind is receptive to scenic beauty (the views are very special), and the day is clear and cool (visibility is very important).

Eastbound, take exit 5 from Interstate 691; at the end of the exit go north (left) on CT 71 about 1 mile to the blue oval Metacomet Trail sign at Cathole Pass. Westbound, take exit 6 from Interstate 691 and follow signs to CT 71, then go north (right) .6 mile to Cathole Pass. There is a small hiker's parking lot with room for two cars cut in behind the trail sign (probably no good in winter). About .1 mile south on the west side of CT 71 there is a pull-out with room for one or two cars. Your route starts up a blue-blazed steep slope that has eroded to its volcanic traprock base.

The leafy green bower over the well-worn path opens a bit as you approach Elmere Reservoir. Swallows gracefully skim its surface in pursuit of tiny flying insects, or to sip water on the wing. After .3 mile, follow the trail across the dam, cross the rocky overflow channel, and continue straight ahead into the woods. If you are lucky and it is the right time of year, you may find a few double-blossomed rue anemones on the dam.

In spring the pink wild geraniums along the trail divert your attention from the solid restful greens that fill the woods. An alcoholic decoction of wild geranium was once used to mitigate the effects of dysentery. Continue along a rocky shaded hillside before dropping right to a dike with a swampy unnamed pond on the left.

One mile from the start the trail emerges on paved Park Drive, which it follows across the dam at the north end of Merimere Reservoir. Here you can enjoy the fine view of the lake and the notch it sits in.

At the dam's end, the trail leads left into the woods. After crossing an attractive rock-bound rill, you edge up the long west side of the reservoir. Then follow near the twisting shore of the lake—the route is peppered with volcanic rocks. After leaving the shore, the way at first is very steep and rocky, but gradually the slope eases and becomes more gradual.

After 2.3 miles, you emerge on cliffs that rise 300 feet above Merimere Reservoir. Evergreen-covered Mine Island below you seems lifted from the Maine Coast. Gerry first saw this island in the early 1960s on an autumn morning as the ground fog was just lifting. Some sights plant themselves so firmly in your mind's eye that they are always there to delight you. You may carefully walk round left onto a cozy rock ledge some ten feet below the cliff's rim.

South Mountain rises from the far shore of the reservoir and Mount Higby's northern cliffs peep up at left (see Hike 29). On the far left you can make out the jagged Hartford skyline.

As you continue uphill along the cliff, several unmarked paths on the left lead to similar viewpoints with slightly different perspectives; all are spectacular on a clear day. One last lookout provides a glimpse of Castle Crag's tower. You follow the blue-blazed trail across a final dip before arriving at the base of Castle Crag's tower (2.6 miles from the start). Climb the tower on rusting steps for a panoramic view.

The vista west is blocked by West Peak. Sleeping Giant (see Hike 49) and West Rock lie to the south and the Metacomet ridges to the north. The white structure on one of these ridges is the Heublein Tower (see Hike 37) and the large building to its right is the University of Connecticut Medical Center in Farmington. In the far distance you can see the east-facing cliffs of Mount Tom in Massachusetts, the Connecticut River gap, and the humps of the Holyoke Range.

Leaving the tower, continue on the blue-blazed trail across the parking lot. Be careful here; your route can be hard to locate. The trail goes across the near corner of the lot and continues up the slope near the cliffs. The route crosses more open cliffs and then drops down almost to the tower's access road.

Just before the road, an alternate descending blue trail that avoids road walking by way of a series of ups-and-downs bears left away from the road.

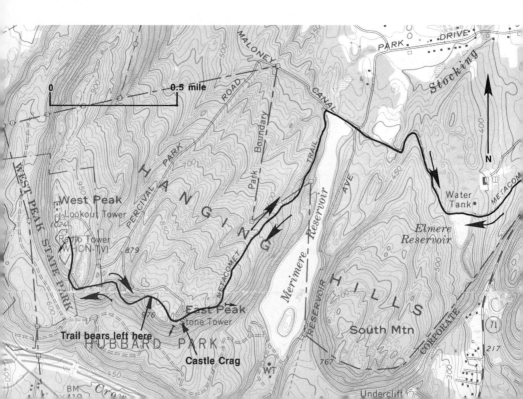

Castle Crag

Take this trail and at the bottom turn right on a tote road. Soon turn right again, slabbing diagonally left up an overgrown scree slope. Bear right and ascend a very attractive draw. Great traprock boulders are "flowing" down the intersection of the scree slopes. Look back—the sides of the draw frame the Sleeping Giant with his head to the right.

Near the top of this draw is a large elderberry bush and a stand of American yew. This is the largest, most southerly batch that we have encountered. The yew's range is listed as New England, so this may be one of its most southerly stands.

The trail levels before bearing left up the steep side a short way to the plateau top of West Peak. Here in June of 1921, the Connecticut Chapter of the Appalachian Mountain Club was formed. They have had at least two reunions here since then, including one marking its sixtieth anniversary in June of 1981. At this point you are 4.1 miles from Cathole Pass. Follow the old road (that you emerge onto) left to a fenced rocky point. You can see the Tunxis ridge to the west. Several cliffs and headlands invite your careful exploration.

After a leisurely lunch—the surrounding thickets make nice spots for a nap—retrace your steps to your car.

Housatonic Range

Total Distance: 7.3 miles
Time: 4 hours
Rating: B
Highlights: Views, rock scrambling
Map: USGS 7½' New Milford

If scrambling over rocks and boulders interests you, here is your hike. This section of the Housatonic Range Trail does not require special rock-climbing skills and technology, but it does have two challenging rock jumbles that demand careful use of both hands.

Remember that the Housatonic Range Trail depends on the deportment of the general public for its continued existence, as no state forest or parks protect this path. Built and maintained by volunteers, the entire trail lies on private land, and irate property owners could close the trail at any time. Do your bit to prevent this from happening by discouraging vandalism, picking up litter, staying on the trail, and greeting landowners pleasantly when passing through.

Candlewood Lake lies to the south of Candlewood Mountain. This 5,420-acre body of water, the largest in the state, has a depth of 85 feet and supports both trout and warm-water fish. Almost all lakes in the state were either created or enlarged by artificial impoundments. Candlewood is composed of several lakes which were joined by an impoundment.

Watch for clumps of Dutchman's

breeches in early spring. The yellow and white flowers look like old-fashioned pantaloons hanging upside down to dry.

From the junction of US 202 and US 7 in Milford, drive north almost 3 miles to CT 37, a left turn off US 7. Watch for the blue trail just before you reach the junction with Candlewood Mountain Road—there is parking for a few cars at the trailhead. This is not the same hike that appeared in earlier editions as the trail has undergone substantial changes due to quarrying and landowner concerns.

South of CT 37 there is now a loop hike of 3.65 miles starting at the parking area. After about .3 miles the trail splits at the loop sign. Take the new trail to the east (left) and continue south passing the side trail to Kelly Slide before climbing Candlewood Mountain (991 ft.) after 2.2 miles. Shortly start a long steady descent. After about .2 mile a short loop trail heads off to the right. This is the very steep Kelly Slide Trail, a ledge sloping to a dropoff which can be dangerously slippery when icy or wet—but there are good views.

Continuing on the main blue-blazed trail, you reach the summit of Pine Knob

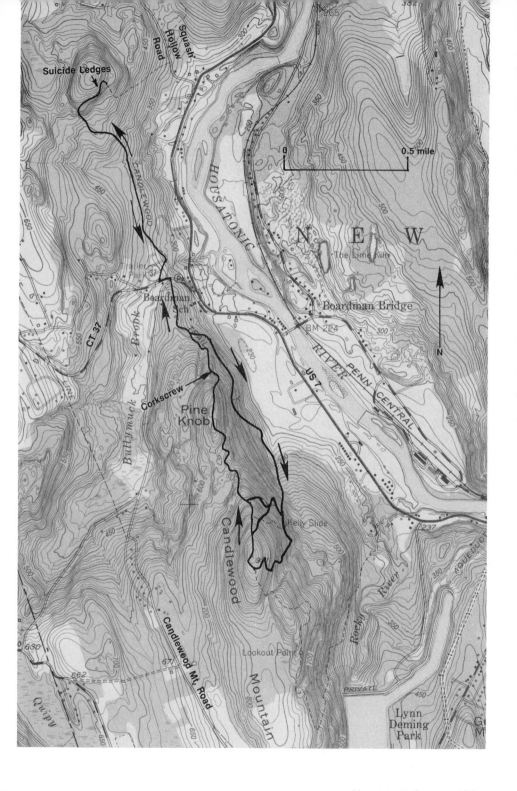

*The Suicide Ledges
on the Housatonic Range*

(one of the many peaks in the state so named) 2.75 miles from the start. Shortly you come to an abrupt drop as the trail descends the Corkscrew. Place your hands and feet carefully while threading your way down this mass of tumbled boulders and steep ledges. After this jumble, proceed on a less steep slope spotted with a few large hemlocks and white pines. Crossing a seasonal runoff, you cut left, up and over more scrambled ledges, and finally drop down to CT 37, .9 mile from Pine Knob.

Turn left on CT 37 and after a bit of road walking proceed right off CT 37 just beyond a trailer park and enter a flat woodland. After a bit you curve left and parallel a stone wall. Forest succession is quite obvious here. The red cedar which first invaded these fields is now being shaded out by the taller, faster-growing hardwoods.

Climb slowly upward through a partially cutover area. After crossing a stream, continue downhill with a stone walk to your left. You reach the great rock mass known as Suicide Ledges about .5 mile from CT 37. The top of the jumble is your destination. Explore the rock caves and find a comfortable spot for a leisurely lunch. Continue on to Squash Hollow Road (another .5 mile). If you choose to return to your car now, you will have hiked about 5.6 miles. We recommend continuing on to the Tories Cave (bring a flashlight) by going left on the road until the trail turns right into the woods. After about .5 mile you reach the Tories Cave Trail at the right. Follow this trail down about .25 mile to the cave. From here retrace your steps to CT 37 where you started.

Sleeping Giant

Total Distance: Option A—5.6 miles; Option B—4.6 miles;
  Option C—9.8 miles
Time: 2 hours, 3½ hours, or 5½ hours
Rating: CB, A, B
Highlights: Views, state park
Maps: USGS 7½' Wallingford, Mount Carmel, Sleeping Giant
  Association Map

Some hikers belittle the size of the Sleeping Giant, for he rises only 700 feet above sea level. They forget he is lying down; were he to awaken and get to his feet, he would stand some two miles tall!

A series of molded and angular volcanic hills just north of New Haven define the shape of the reclining titan. Legend has it that the giant was first recognized and named from sailing ships in New Haven Harbor many years ago. From the various parts of his anatomy you can see numerous peaks and ridges that other hikes in this book traverse. The giant is now contained in a 1,300-acre state park. Only a short distance from downtown New Haven, it is a popular spot with campers, picnickers, and hikers. In 1977 the Sleeping Giant trail system was dedicated as a National Scenic Trail.

From the junction of CT 42 and CT 10, drive south 4.2 miles on CT 10 to the stoplight at Mt. Carmel Avenue. Follow this street left (east) for .3 mile to the park entrance and parking lot. Quinnipiac College is just across the road.

The twenty-eight-mile park trail system designed by Norman Greist and Richard Elliot, key members of the Sleeping Giant Park Association, is ingeniously laid out in a series of loops. No matter how long or short a hike you wish, you need never retrace your steps. Six east-west trails, marked with blue, white, violet, green, orange, and yellow blazes, join the opposite ends of the park. Five north-south trails marked with red diamonds, squares, hexagons, circles, and triangles cut across the park. The loop combinations you may devise seem endless.

We have selected two pairs of trails in Sleeping Giant. Since they start at about the same location you can combine the two for a real leg stretcher. The Connecticut Chapter of the Appalachian Mountain Club has offered all the trails in this state park on a single day for those who really wanted to test their hiking ability!

We favor the blue-white trail combination. It is the most strenuous, covers most of the giant's anatomy, and affords the best views. Start up the right side of the paved picnic loop through the pine-shaded grove. To your right is a cluster of great red oaks. These tall oaks did not "from little acorns grow"; they are stump sprouts from a tree cut long ago. Tree clusters like this one are common in Connecticut's much cut-over woodlands.

Follow the blue-blazed feeder trail to the right towards a gully before cutting left across the hillside. You will soon join the main blue-blazed Quinnipiac Trail, the oldest in Connecticut's blue trail system. Bear right.

Shortly the first ascent takes you onto the giant's elbow. The trail follows the cedar-spotted basalt ridge of his crooked arm to the right, drops down,

and then ascends his head. A quarry falls off steeply to your left. This stretch is a long, difficult scramble—a good test of your hiking condition. (Avoid this area in winter; the slope is usually icy and treacherous.)

Back to the right you will see two ridges. The Quinnipiac Trail runs along the closer mass of shapeless hills; the Regicides' Trail follows the long ridge further right. (The east end of West Rock on the Regicides' Trail offers a particularly good overall perspective of the giant.) The neat lawns and tastefully spaced buildings of Quinnipiac College lie below.

Continue to the jutting cliff of the giant's chin. The wide path in the valley

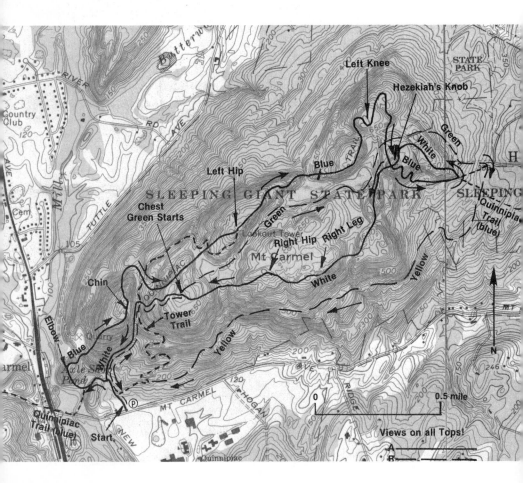

Mountain laurel time in the Giant

below is the Tower Trail; beyond it rises the giant's massive chest. Looking north you can see the traprock ridges known as the Hanging Hills where the Metacomet and Mattabesett Trails join. West Peak, a large rock mass with a crown of towers, lies at the left just beyond the rock tower of Castle Crag (see Hike 47). The flat-topped peak to the right is South Mountain. The city of Meriden fills the break in the ridge; the two hills farthest to the right are Mount Lamentation and Chauncey Peak (see Hike 35). All these basalt peaks and plateaus resulted from lava flows some 200 million years ago.

The trail zigzags steeply down the north end of the giant's head and then climbs his left hip, also known as Mt. Carmel, 1.5 miles from the picnic ground. Perhaps the best view in the park is from the top of the summit tower, a ramped rock structure built by the WPA in the 1930s. The hilly panorama continues east and south; starting with Mount Lamentation, you see the impressive cliff faces of Mount Higby (see Hike 29), the gap through which US 6 passes, and the long ridge of Beseck Mountain. Like the hills to the north, these ridges are traversed by trails. The barrenness of the land makes landowners more willing to give hiking clubs permission to cut trails on hills than on their more fertile property. Fortunately hikers much prefer these barren hills to the low-lying fertile fields.

If you choose only the easier 4.6 mile route (Option B) to reach the beginning of the green trail, follow the tarred circle road serving the picnic area around to the white-blazed trail on your right. This passes over the bridge and crosses a seasonal stream, where it then goes diagonally up the hill. The white-blazed trail reaches and then goes right along the base of a scree slope.

In about .3 mile the white trail crosses the heavily worn Tower Trail. After going a short distance left the white blazes go right into the woods. At last you emerge on the chest with a view of the giant's head and the valley to the south. At a second viewpoint from the giant's chest you will see Quinnipiac College below you.

From this second viewpoint follow the green blazes left (the white blazes continue straight). The green trail crosses the park to the north side of the central spine. During the peregrinations of the trail, your path crosses many of the various north-south red-blazed trails.

If you choose the proper time and year, the mountain laurel display will be magnificent. Almost your entire route is graced with these crag-loving bushes.

It becomes more and more obvious as you proceed that you are on an old tote road. Toward the east end of the park (you may have heard cars and glimpsed electric wires through the trees), the green blazes go right into the woods. In just a few yards you come to a great meeting point where all the east-west trails converge.

Go back to the yellow blazes. Proceed left into the woods before the yellow trail straightens out and parallels the rest of the east-west trails. Even though this route is easier than most in the park, the numerous ups and downs and rough rocky footing make it fairly tough. A few red "symbol" trails cross your path, but otherwise it is refreshingly uneventful and very quiet until within earshot of Mt. Carmel Avenue. Near the end, our route was blocked by the upper part of a fallen hemlock, blasted by lightning. The force of this electrical charge was so powerful it not only vaporized the sap, which lifted the bark along its path, but snapped the tree completely off.

Soon the yellow-blazed trail joins a dirt road that goes left and continues to the beginning of the picnic circle where you go left to reach your car.

If you prefer the 9.8 mile option — which combines the loops described in options A and B — as you head west on the white trail and reach the giant's chest, follow the green trail east from the junction of the white and green trails.

The trail continues to the cliff edge, where you can look south to the giant's right hip, right leg, and right knee before dropping down to the right. After a level spell through white pines, the trail drops and then ascends his left leg. It dips again and goes up the left knee. Note the pitting produced by centuries of exposure on the weathered rocks; they contrast sharply with the smooth faces of a few nearby recently uncovered rock surfaces.

Working down the far end of the giant's knee, you encounter the first section of smooth, rolling, rock-free trail. Footing makes a tremendous difference in hiking difficulty and the angular volcanic-rock ridges of central Connecticut are particularly treacherous. The size of the dogwood here attests to the rich depth of the soil beneath them.

Begin your ascent of Hezekiah's Knob. As you near the top (3.2 miles from the start), look to the right for early spring-blooming purple and white hepaticas with their characteristic three-lobed leaves left over from the previous summer's growth. The leaf's shape, supposedly like a liver, was the basis for its medicinal use for various liver problems.

The blue and white trails meet on the knob. You can return on the white trail now or continue a bit further on the giant's right foot at the park's far end. The blue trail describes a long zigzag down the slope. At the next junction, bear left with the green and blue blazes. In a few yards, turn left again onto the white-blazed trail to climb his right foot. From the summit the trail drops down to a wet area, which you pass over on strategically placed stepping stones before ascending Hezekiah's Knob again.

Proceed straight down the hill on the white trail. When you reach the top of his right knee, look north across the valley to the giant's rocky left side where you hiked earlier. The trail leads down the stone-strewn slope and then up and down his right leg and right hip. The red triangle trail cuts across the park by the base of the sleeping titan's chest—this path has the last climb of this circuit. The trail winds up around the great boulders. In spring you may hear a stream echoing somewhere in the hollows beneath you.

White and green blazes mark the route here. With a last look at tiny Quinnipiac College below the giant's head across the way, you twist down off his chest on the white trail and join the Tower Trail for a short distance. The path leaves the road at right to follow a course tucked under the giant's chin to the picnic area. At the paved road, head left for the shortest route back to your car.

Ratlum Mountain and Indian Caves

Total Distance: 13 miles
Time: 8 hours
Rating: B
Highlights: Reservoir views, Indian Council caves
Map: USGS 7½′ New Hartford

Although Connecticut does not have great bodies of water like those in New Hampshire's lakes region or the Great Lakes, we once had many lakes, compliments of the Ice Age. Most of those left have had their levels raised by dams, and many new lakes have been created by damming streams and rivers. Still, bodies of water are transient. Natural succession proceeds from a lake or pond, to marsh or swamp, to meadow, and, ultimately, to forest. Connecticut is dotted with large swampy areas that were once lakes and ponds. These continuing processes have occurred over the last 10,000 years since the glaciers retreated.

By building dams we have temporarily increased our water acreage greatly, but we have only pushed nature back a few hundred, or at most, a few thousand years. Even as we push, nature continues to drop tons of alluvium and rotting vegetation into our lakes and ponds each year. The life of any body of water is dependent on many factors, including the size of inlet streams, the volume of silt/m³ of the water, the depth, and the nutrients in the incoming water, which govern the growth rate of water vegetation.

Some of man's actions greatly accelerate the filling of the bodies of water that we go to so much trouble and expense to create. Road cuts, developments, and poor farming practices continually supply lake-filling silt. Often the fertilizers put on farm fields and lawns enhance the growth of choking vegetation in our bodies of water. This hike passes many bodies of water at various stages of succession; no doubt some are now unrecognizable to the layman's eyes.

Drive to the junction of CT 219 and CT 179 in Barkhamsted. Go north on CT 179 one mile to a gated old town road on the left (west) just opposite Legeyt Road. There is room to park on the right off the road. Do not block the gated road.

Go through the gate and follow the old road as it passes through Metropolitan District Commission land. At the start, you pass several white birch trees with their peeling bark and oval leaves; however, a single, tall, grey birch arches over the right side of the road. With its tight bark, large black triangles under its branches, and triangular leaves, this is a very different tree. A good way to learn to distinguish between similar trees is to find two species growing near one another. The white birch is considered a tree of the north although a few are found in northern Connecticut. On the other hand, the grey birch, while not common in northern New England, is found naturally as far south as Big Meadows (VA) in Shenandoah National Park.

Just before a shallow pond at left we found a clump of pearly everlasting—flat clusters of round white flowers with a dull yellow center, which are popular with dried flower enthusiasts. This is another northern species; sweet everlasting is more common in Connecticut.

At the bottom of a small hill, there is another small pond at left in the later stages of returning to the land. Try to visualize its original clear beauty. Now it is much smaller; trees are growing in its once open water, especially on the shallower inlet side. Submerged and emergent vegetation is adding to decay—as the pond becomes shallower its rate of filling increases. In a few hundred years, someone may cross this area cussing the swampy wetness underfoot!

Opposite this pond, the blue-blazed Tunxis Trail goes off to the right on its way north to the Massachusetts border. Continue on the old road, now blue-blazed, until still another pond appears at left; our trail goes off to the right and climbs up through the Indian Council Caves. These are huge boulders used by the Native Americans as a gathering place. Circle left up and around this rock jumble to a lookout on top with views of the surrounding forests. You are now on the Tunxis Trail heading south to Ratlum Mountain.

Follow the blue blazes through this typical northern Connecticut forest over ledges and through laurel, crossing two small streams before reaching the wider Kettle Brook about one mile from the caves (two miles from the start). Cross Kettle Brook on the dirt road, turn left into the woods with the blue blazes, and climb gradually through hemlocks. Enjoy the soft forest floor underfoot here. Cross a dirt road and pass through a small field thick with goldenrod. Soon the trail (now an old road) crosses a small brook and climbs steadily through mixed laurel and birch. Our trail bears right off the old road, climbs to a rock ledge, joins another old road, turns right and soon zigzags up yet another rock ledge. Although it has no views, this is the highest place around (1,180 feet). Follow the blue blazes downhill, cross a

Barkhamsted Reservoir from Ratlum Mountain

woods road, and then cross a stone wall by an immense spreading oak tree. Continue on the blue-blazed trail, reaching CT 219 about three miles from the start.

Cross CT 219, enter the woods, and climb gradually through laurel. Our trail is well-marked and obvious here—people have been cutting firewood in this area. Be careful to follow the blue blazes as there are many woods roads traversing this section. Cross a brook and pass a clump of four white birches at left before reaching paved Ratlum

Road in just under a mile.

Go left uphill on Ratlum Road for about 50 feet and then right into the woods. Climb uphill through the woods, soon reaching a lookout with fine views of Barkhamsted Reservoir to the west and northwest. Continue along the edge of the cliff and then through nearly level woods passing a yellow trail going left about 1.5 miles from the road. This is one of three yellow-blazed trails that go east off the Tunxis Trail between Ratlum Road and Lookout Point. We suspect that all three go to an extension of Rat-

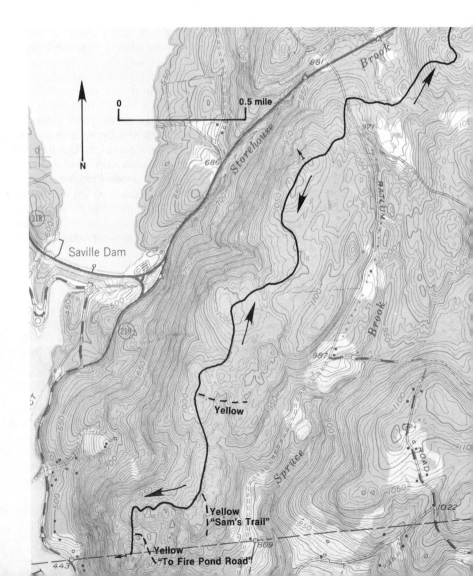

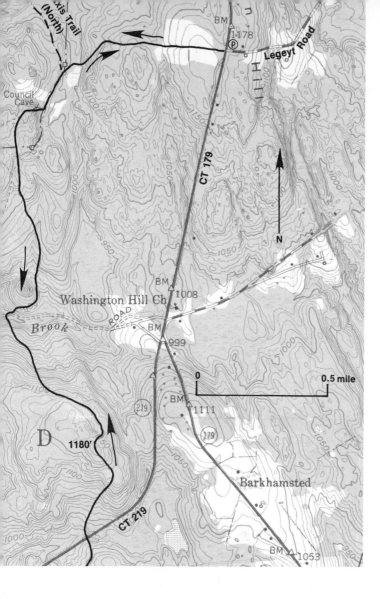

lum Road. After another .5 mile of nearly level walking, you will pass the second yellow-blazed trail with a sign saying "SAM'S TRAIL."

Proceed over an overgrown rocky top, zigzag down and then up, again passing the third yellow-blazed trail after another half-mile. Here there is a sign, "To Fire Pond Road." Stay on the blue-blazed Tunxis Trail south and shortly

you reach Lookout Point (1,000 feet) about 6.5 miles from the your car. This is an ideal lunch spot with fine views of Compensating Reservoir.

After enjoying the view, retrace your steps to your car. Pause to admire the evergreen, a trailing arbutus (may-flower), between the second and third yellow trails on your return.

Books from The Countryman Press
and Backcountry Publications

Written for people of all ages and experience, these popular and carefully prepared books feature detailed trail and tour directions, notes on points of interest and natural highlights, maps, and photographs.

Hiking Series:

Fifty Hikes in the Adirondacks, Second Edition $13.00
Fifty Hikes in Central New York, $12.00
Fifty Hikes in Central Pennsylvania, Second Edition $12.00
Fifty Hikes in Connecticut, Third Edition $12.00
Fifty Hikes in Eastern Pennsylvania, Second Edition $12.00
Fifty Hikes in the Hudson Valley, Second Edition, $14.00
Fifty Hikes in Lower Michigan, $13.00
Fifty Hikes in Massachusetts, Second Edition $13.00
Fifty Hikes in New Jersey, $13.00
Fifty Hikes in Northern Maine, $12.00
Fifty Hikes in Northern Virginia, $13.00
Fifty Hikes in Ohio, $12.95
Fifty Hikes in Southern Maine, $10.95
Fifty Hikes in Vermont, Fourth Edition $12.00
Fifty Hikes in Western New York, $13.00
Fifty Hikes in Western Pennsylvania, Second Edition $12.00
Fifty Hikes in the White Mountains, Fourth Edition $13.00
Fifty More Hikes in New Hampshire, $13.00

Walks & Rambles Series

Walks & Rambles in Dutchess and Putnam Counties, $11.00
Walks & Rambles in Westchester and Fairfield Counties, Second Edition $11.00
Walks & Rambles on the Delmarva Peninsula, $11.00
Walks & Rambles in the Upper Connecticut River Valley, $10.00
Walks & Rambles on Cape Cod and the Islands, $11.00
Walks & Rambles in Rhode Island, $11.00
More Walks & Rambles in Rhode Island, $11.00

Our titles are available in bookshops and in many sporting goods stores, or they may be ordered directly from the publisher. Shipping and handling costs are $2.50 for 1-2 books, $3 for 3-6 books, and $3.50 for 7 or more books. To order, or for a complete catalog, please write to:

The Countryman Press, Inc.
PO Box 175
Woodstock, VT 05091
or call our toll-free number, (800) 245-4151.